WIRRAL
MEMORIES

The publishers would like to thank the following companies for their

support in the production of this book

Main Sponsor
Lees & Partners Solicitors

British Sub-Aqua Club

Cabot Carbon Limited

Charles Stephens Funeral Directors

Moorcroft Construction Ltd

Pyramids Shopping Centre

Roberts & Company

Staniford (Rock Ferry) Ltd

T E Hughes & Son Ltd

Vauxhall Motors Ltd

First published in Great Britain by True North Books Limited
England HX3 6AE
01422 344344

ISBN 1 903204 74 7

Text, design and origination by True North Books Limited
Printed and bound by Martins The Printers

WIRRAL
MEMORIES

Contents

Introduction

Looking back at the events that helped shape modern society and its attitudes is an exercise that is not just for the oldies amongst us. Younger readers can also share in a form of secondary nostalgia as they relive the times in which their parents and grandparents grew up. When we do sit down and examine what has happened to our lives over the last couple of generations it is remarkable to realise how different things are today in lifestyle and all that we see about us. Even in a single lifetime of the traditional three score years and ten, there has been so much upheaval. 'Wirral Memories' takes us through that period by focussing on the middle years of the last century, highlighting places, people, buildings and events of significance. The use of delightful photographs and pithy, thought provoking captions help some readers revisit a few of those that may have been forgotten or can only sketchily remember. For others the scenes depicted may be completely new and they will come to them with only a secondhand knowledge, having gleaned their information from older members of the family. As the reader delves further into the book a flavour of the recent past, in general historical terms, should come through. Perhaps 'Wirral Memories' will settle a few arguments or, better still, provoke more discussion about the area we love and think we know so well.

This book about the Wirral does not concentrate on any single town, though the larger settlements obviously feature prominently. It tries to give examples of life in the smaller districts of the region in order to retain a balance in providing a flavour of village and more rural community activity as well as that in the built up areas. Going much further back in time, the Wirral did not have its major centres of population. Defined as that part of Britain bounded by the River Mersey, Irish Sea and River Dee, what is now a metropolitan district of Merseyside had been, in Saxon times, a mixture of woodland and open spaces, with a scattering of small farms, cottages and fishermen's huts. The only real link with the outside world was via a track that led from the Mersey to Chester. It was from Chester that Benedictine monks used to travel to Liverpool

in order to trade with its merchants, using a ferry at the river's narrowest point to cross the water. The name of Monk's Ferry lives on today. Making such a journey on a daily basis was time consuming and uneconomic, so in about 1150, they built a priory at Birkenhead. The place name was probably derived from 'Birchenhead', relating to the birch trees nearby or possibly the head of the River Birch or Birkett. The priory was an important building and from there the monks established a public ferry service in 1330. It was originally free, but eventually a charge was levied as demand outgrew their expectations. A community sprang up around the priory, the forerunner of the modern Birkenhead.

The peninsula was mentioned in the Domesday Book, but there was little national interest in the region until Edward II granted the ferry charter. Even after the Benedictines had become established, there was little change in the lives of most people on the Wirral. Although the priory was used as a garrison in the 17th century during the Civil War, life generally passed by and locals were left alone to continue as a mainly agricultural society.

Then the 19th century dawned and cathartic change came to the Wirral. This was the time of the industrial revolution and the beginning of the end for the traditional way of life on the land that the majority of people had experienced for countless generations. Steam powered ferry boats were introduced on the Mersey and they helped open up the Wirral as a desirable spot from where wealthy merchants and businessmen could commute to an overcrowded Liverpool. It was only a short step from there to establishing companies on this side of the river. John Laird was one of those who seized his opportunity and, in 1824, built a boiler and ironworks in Birkenhead. This was the embryo of what would become the internationally famous Cammell Laird shipyards. In 1847 Wallasey Pool was converted into docks that would eventually cover six miles of quayside. The coming of the railway helped the Wirral expand even more as opportunity to access markets by land as well as sea was provided. Other industries came to this newly flourishing district, including a mammoth flour milling plant, the largest in the world, and, in 1860, Lever's soap and detergent works.

Heavy industry attracted large numbers of labourers who left their homes in other parts of the country as well as the rural Wirral farms and settled in Wallasey and Birkenhead, expanding those settlements into towns. Laird laid out

Birkenhead's town centre in its grid pattern and the Town Hall and Market Hall were built. An official population of about 100 in 1800 had exploded to reach over 40,000 by the middle of the 19th century. A railway tunnel under the Mersey made the Wirral even more accessible, but life was not all about factory chimneys and ocean going ships. There were some who gave consideration to more pleasing sights. Joseph Paxton was one such person. He was the superintendent of the Duke of Devonshire's estate at Chatsworth and he drew on his landscaping experience in designing Birkenhead Park. The world's first municipal park was created by draining marshland and laying down sports pitches, driveways, artificial lakes and involved the use of generous landscaping. His work finished in 1847 and Paxton went on to help design the Houses of Parliament and the Crystal Palace.

By the time the last century opened the Wirral had changed dramatically from a sleepy country and coastal region to one of thriving activity. How that developed from the depression of the interwar years through to the start of consumerism in the late 1970s can be seen in elements of 'Wirral Memories'. It is not intended to be a historical tome, but one that will allow the reader to indulge in flights of fancy and indulge in nostalgia for what are described by many as 'the good old days'. However, it is up to the individual to judge the accuracy of that statement. What is certain is that we can, with the help of the images on the following pages, drive once more along Birkenhead's Grange Road, enjoy a show at New Brighton's Tower Theatre, swim in the open air baths at Hoylake and stroll safely through Wallasey Village after hours. You are about to return to times when opposing football supporters stood side by side on the terraces at Prenton Park without punching one another, when a gentleman offered his seat on a bus to a lady without being asked 'What's your game, then?' and when children said, 'Good morning, sir' to the headmaster and not 'Hiya' to the headteacher. 'Wirral Memories' will make you reach for a penny Arrow bar to chew on, a bottle of Corona lemonade to drink and a Craven 'A' fag to pull on for 'your throat's sake'. Listen to Uncle Mac on the wireless as he introduces Sparky's 'Magic piano' or chuckle at Mrs Mopp asking Tommy Handley, 'Can I do you now, sir?' Get in the mood to enjoy that trip down memory lane that lies ahead as you turn the page.

Street Scenes

Below: Judy Garland immortalised the humble tram in her 'Trolley Song', performed in the 1944 movie 'Meet me in St Louis'. By then, it was too late for the Wirral. The last one clanked its final way along the track in the summer of 1937. This one, decked out in rather jolly fashion considering it was attending its own funeral, was outside Woodside Station. The lettering reminded the public that the service had been operating for 77 years. Originally, the power to drive the cars was provided by horses and our tramway was the first one to be operated anywhere in Europe. The inaugural journey from Birkenhead Park to the ferry at Woodside was a transport landmark. The lines were electrified in 1901, but investment in new rolling stock ceased just before the start of World War I. It is ironic to think that Birkenhead had already considered phasing out the service so long ago, yet a number of cities have started to reintroduce trams to their streets in recent years. The last route in operation was on the Oxton-Claughton circle and the final journey took place on 17 July 1937. They may have been draughty and a little noisy, but trams were part of our heritage and their place in transport museums always attracts crowds of fascinated visitors.

Left: Rock Lane runs from Dacre Hill down to Rock Ferry, where the oil terminal now stands. This pictured section is the western part of the road that lies between the old and new Chester Roads. One of Rock Ferry's claims to fame is that it was once home to the influential American writer, Nathaniel Hawthorne, during his time as his country's consul in Liverpool, 1853-57. When he came to England his reputation as an outstanding author had been established by the publication of his best received novel, 'The Scarlet Letter', in 1850. He would have loved the leafy lanes and gentle pace of life that changed little on this road in the intervening years between his residency and this view from the following century. He would have used the ferry, in common with many others, as a convenient means of commuting to and from Liverpool. Hawthorne lived at Rock Park and his house was typical of the grand residences favoured by professional people, merchants and other well to do members of the middle classes. Squeezed of its lifeblood by the Mersey Tunnel, the ferry closed in 1939. By then, those of the monied classes drove themselves into the city, regarding travel by public transport where they mixed with the common herd as being beneath them.

The Walpamur depot, on the right, offered the DIY enthusiast plenty of scope for paint and wallpaper to brighten up his prewar living room. The eagle eyed can date this scene fairly accurately as there is plenty of evidence in the makes and models of the cars we can observe. There is also the clue to be taken from the women's fashion and a further one from the age of the pram the young mum is pushing along the pavement on Grange Road West. But, the best guess can be made using the road markings in the foreground. There is a pair of Belisha beacons on the opposite kerbs that owe their name to the Minister for Transport (1934-37), Leslie Hore-Belisha. He introduced the pedestrian crossings into

London in the first year of office and, by 1935, they had become common in most towns. The zebra style road markings were added some years later and, initially, drivers had to be vigilant in their spotting of the pavement based beacons and studs on the carriageway. Road safety became a major issue for the government, with a raft of measures being introduced to make our streets safer as car ownership rose by 20 per cent in the mid 1930s. The driving test was brought in, the use of dipped headlights in the dark made compulsory and a 30 mph speed limit set in built up areas in March 1935. Somewhat ludicrously, police were supposed to stop speeding motorists by sounding a gong fitted to their vehicles.

Below: The ferry terminal at Seacombe, photographed in 1952, was just one of ten such places from where travellers could embark across the river in Victorian times. How busy those links between the Wirral and Liverpool must have been as the Mersey was crossed and recrossed by scores of boats packed to the gunwales with passengers. A service had been in operation at Seacombe from as far back as the middle of the 17th century. By the 1920s some 32 million people were carried each year on the 10 minute journey, a staggering statistic that reinforces the importance of the ferry service to the daily life of so many. The floating landing stage, with huge tyres chained to its edge to act as buffers, was an impressive sight as gulls whirled overhead, calling their plaintive cries to the throngs waiting below. Seacombe was a busy shipbuilding centre in the mid 1800s, but it is the ferry by which it is widely known. When Gerry Marsden and his Pacemakers first began singing 'Ferry across the Mersey' and up the pop charts in 1964, this was the one that provided the inspiration. Although now principally tourist attractions, Seacombe and Woodside ferries survive as a reminder of their place in local transport history.

Above: How many of those out and about on foot or in cars knew that Wallasey could trace its recorded history back to Norman times? Then a hamlet, its name appears in the Domesday Book. It was part of the land owned by Robert of Rhuddlan, North Wales and mention was also made of Robert's influence over Meols, Thuraston and Heswall. It is not quite Piccadilly Circus, but Wallasey's Liscard roundabout had enough

people in its vicinity to suggest that you were bound to meet someone you knew. The pretty flowers in their well tended beds were a credit to council gardeners as they provided an attractive backdrop to the pedestrians going about their business under the shop awnings and along the pavements. Some 45 years ago the motor car was still a welcome sight on the roads, though ownership increased considerably as the austerity of the postwar years was thrown aside. Britain entered the 1950s still attempting to recover from a crippling war debt and with an urgent need to rebuild industries and housing lost to enemy action. Rationing of many High Street commodities was still in force and many muttered that winning the peace was more difficult than winning the war. What a difference a few years can make, because by the end of the 1950s we were all smiles again.

Corporation Road, connecting Hoylake Road with Vittoria Dock, seems now to be a series of roundabouts of one form or another where busy traffic tries to keep moving in the hurly burly of the 20th century. It was far from quiet 50 years ago, but the pace and style of movement come from a time when dad was but a lad. On 22 October 1953 the cobbled street was just as likely to echo to the clip clop of a coalman's or rag and bone man's horse as it pulled the cart gently on its way. A policeman on the street corner had the time to chat with a local resident who knew him to be a friendly upholder of law and order. The billboards on the wall of the Vittoria café were simple adverts for products that lacked the 'in your face' aggression of modern marketing. Some of them have disappeared into the mists of time, but others continue to flourish much as they ever did. Does anyone remember Three Threes, but who has never heard of Smarties? Some things never change whereas others are lost forever. Note that few chimney stacks were adorned with even television aerials, never mind satellite dishes. The gogglebox was still in its infancy and few homes could afford one, though there had been an upsurge in sales around the time of the Queen's coronation a few months earlier.

Below: As children many of us played on bomb sites in the late 1940s and early 1950s. They were not the safest of places, with their rubble and glass shards still lying around in abundance, but at least they were a form of open space where children could enjoy themselves. Closer to town and city centres they were used as car parks before the redevelopers found the time and money to indulge in the rebuilding and regeneration that was so badly needed after the war. Yet, it all took a while to be fully achieved and, in some spots, longer than most. Certain buildings lay derelict for years, as can be seen here since demolition work was yet to be completed well over a decade after the declaration of peace. While this may seem that there was some dragging of feet, we must appreciate the mammoth task that faced Birkenhead and its surrounding areas. Merseyside was the second largest enemy target after London during World War II as the docks and surrounding districts felt the might of aerial bombardment. The worst periods were during the heavy blitzes that began in August 1940, continuing almost unabated until November 1941. Some 355 fatalities were recorded in Wallasey and 464 in Birkenhead, with 200 of the latter taking place on the terrible night of 12 March 1941. Overall, in Birkenhead 2,000 homes were completely destroyed, with countless thousands of others damaged. The picture was mirrored across the rest of Merseyside.

Above: Argyle Street South, stretching down towards Borough Road, would have some similarities with those long, straight French avenues were it not for the property that fronted it. Instead of rows of trees, we have terraced housing sweeping down the hill. Some of the older buildings we can see made way for the flyover in a move that was mooted as an improvement scheme. Certainly the housing belonged to an outdated era, but its demolition meant radical changes in lifestyle for a lot of the former residents. They were used to their own little bit of England that was also part of a vibrant community. It was easy to get along with neighbours who were literally on the doorstep, especially if they had run out of sugar and appeared with a cup requesting a brief loan. Children called adults 'uncle' or 'aunty' across the backyard wall and everyone kept an eye out for the other. When these families moved to high rise flats or large council estates much of the bond that held a small community together seems to have been broken. In this case big was not necessarily beautiful. Anyone gazing down Argyle Street South today would take in a lot more than a lonely motorbike parked at the kerb as traffic levels have escalated over the last 50 years.

Below: The Birkenhead Brewery dray brought its load to the Commercial Hotel on the corner of Grange Road and Tunnel Road. Barrels were rolled down the chute and into the cellar, after which many a drayman would enjoy a relaxing pint with the landlord before moving off to the next pub on his schedule. But there was a snag to this common practice. Barbara Castle, the Minister of Transport in the mid 1960s, had just introduced the breathalyser as a road safety feature. While a necessary step forward in bringing common sense to bear on some motorists' habits, it helped change the habits of a lifetime. The drive out to the country pub became less attractive if there was to be a danger of policemen lurking in lay-bys ready to pounce. Taxi firms rubbed their hands with glee at the increase in business, but the draymen cursed loud and long about the removal of their perks. The milk stout being sold at the Commercial puts us in mind of the three old ladies in the snug of the Rovers' Return on ITV's 'Coronation Street'. It was the favourite tipple of Ena, Martha and Minnie, but its association with pensioners meant that anyone under the age of 60 would not be seen dead asking for a bottle of this brew by name.

A deserted roundabout at Charing Cross in the early 1960s, looking towards Atherton Street. How this part of Birkenhead has changed since then. Now we have fast food shops and the Pyramids to catch our eye instead of a quiet thoroughfare. This decade was the last of what we might call the old days. The 1970s brought us the revolution in town centre planning when architecture went out of the window and convenience swept in. Gone are the pretty cornices, lovely cupolas and carved, decorative facades. In their stead we got concrete, steel and glass built in uniform rectangular shapes, almost completely devoid of character, but very functional. In the swinging 60s we could balance the old and the new. Young people had more of a say in life as their spending power brought greater recognition, but they were not the ones who demanded a change to the face of our towns. They were more interested in altering music and fashion or, for the more serious minded, in changing attitudes to women, ethnic minorities and aggression. The baby boomers found their voices, burned their bras and helped shift entrenched opinions. What a pity that they could not influence the plans of the architects and developers to the same degree.

Right: The Ford Cortina was one of the doyens of motor manufacturing in the 1960s and 70s and the model parked along Grange Road was a good example of a car that had joined the senior ranks of popularity on salesroom forecourts. The decade that was coming to an end had been an exciting one, particularly for the younger generation. It is remarkable that the youth of today seem to be more aware of the music and fashions beloved of their parents than we ever were of those our mums and dads favoured. If we were in our 20s in the 1960s we had little interest in the showy musicals that Busby Berkeley brought to the cinema, the crooning of the old groaner, Bing Crosby, the fact that Portsmouth won the last FA Cup Final before war broke out or the length of our mothers' hemlines. Yet, young people now are very familiar with 'Carry on' films, the music of the Beatles, the 1966 World Cup and Mary Quant's miniskirts. Are they just better informed than we were or is this proof of the major influence the swinging 60s had on British lifestyle? Of course, we older ones know the answer and we are not averse to sharing that view with all and sundry.

Below: Scott's self service store was a sign of the times in 1967. Occupying a prominent place on Birkenhead's Grange Road, the lettering on the shop front was a positive statement of its determination to modernise and meet the challenge of the supermarket full on. The days of a myriad of little individual shops were numbered. As the pile 'em high, sell 'em cheap brigade made its influence known, the pressure on the small man was too much for many to bear. Although some could survive, shoppers no longer came along in the droves that would allow several butchers or greengrocers to flourish in proximity to one another. Those that did remain had to fight that bit harder for custom and some shops like Scott's went over to self service. This allowed more goods to be out on show and gave housewives greater choice when carrying out their weekly shop. It also meant that the personal touch became something of the past. Where shopkeepers had once chatted away to their customers as ham was sliced or potatoes weighed out, they now just emptied the wire baskets, rang up the chosen items on the till and popped the cash into the drawer. Shopping became quicker, but more functional and less of a social occasion.

Bottom: The area around Randle Street, as viewed from Mersey Park flats, had, c1970, been earmarked for demolition. The terraced housing behind Birkenhead's Park Motors was typical of the style of homes in which many of us grew up. Back yards opened onto alleyways that ran the length of the terrace. Along there budding soccer stars honed their skills by dribbling a tennis ball up and down, playing literal wall passes against the brickwork as they did so. Girls turned skipping ropes or played two ball to the accompaniment of traditional rhymes about Matthew, Mark, Luke and John as mum kept her front step bright and sparkling with the vigorous use of a donkeystone. Living conditions were cramped and neighbours seemed to live almost on top of each other, but that helped a true community spirit to develop. Although everyone knew each other's business, there was a commonality of purpose and real sense of sharing in both success and woe for the inhabitants of these back streets. They defended their territory with a togetherness that was lost when people were encouraged to move to the impersonal high rise flats that became home to many in the 1960s and 1970s. Children could no longer step over the threshold to play their street games and mothers had no opportunity to stand on their front steps and gossip about the hoity-toity woman at number three with her net curtains and airs and graces.

Below: This section of Oxton Road, Birkenhead shows nos 20-54 as they looked 30 or so years ago. Even then, traffic restriction measures had come into force. No entry signs, one way streets and the dreaded yellow lines abounded in the conspiracy against the humble motorist. A few isolated free parking bays gave him some little oasis in the desert of red tape and by-laws, but you would be hard pressed to find many of those in evidence today. This was the beginning of the concerted effort to discourage traffic in our town centres. The spiralling growth in car ownership meant that everyone, it seemed, wanted to come to work or go shopping using his own transport. There was no doubling up of passengers and it was commonplace to see just one person in a car. The multi-storey car park came into being, but there was little attempt made by our administrators to improve public transport to a degree that would encourage motorists to seek alternative ways of travelling into town. It seems as if the problem is insoluble, because despite bus lanes, pedestrianised shopping areas, high parking charges and other discouragement to drivers there has been little or no improvement to the congested state of our roads.

Right: With Midland Street to the left and Tetbury Street to the right, the zebra crossing is roughly halfway along Oxton Road, running from the junction with Balls Road to Grange Road shopping area. Despite some redevelopment further back at Town View, the scene around 56-70 Oxton Road is much the same as in 1971. The only difference might be that the various premises look that bit older and more down at heel than they did over 30 years ago. Even the newer flats have not succeeded in brightening up this part of Birkenhead. Further down the road, as the redeveloped shopping area is reached, the scene is much brighter and is a constant hubbub of busy noise and lively activity. The baby in the pram on the crossing, now halfway through his allotted life span, has grown up in a time of great change. Men walked on the moon regularly when he was a toddler. Whilst at primary school he witnessed the first woman to take charge of 10 Downing Street and, as he sat his GCSEs, he heard of the devastation that the nuclear age could wreak when the Chernobyl reactor malfunctioned. He saw DNA develop as a major forensic tool, computers becoming established in the workplace and then the home and the dubious merits of cloning. None of all this made much difference to Oxton Road.

Above right: This was the view of the new shopping precinct site as seen from the top of Beattie's roof in 1972. How the proprietors of the small, individual shops around here must have trembled at the thought of having to compete with the chain stores and better appointed retail outlets that would

soon be in place. Many tried to struggle on and some succeeded in surviving, but for others enough was enough and they called it a day. Shoppers were no longer willing to traipse from one part of town to another in order to fill their bags when there was an opportunity to do the lot under one roof. As time went by and supermarkets branched out into clothing and other goods in addition to food, it was possible to do all the shopping in a single store. Parked by the kerbside below the photographer is a string of British built cars. Now that places the photograph firmly in the nostalgic bracket. The wave of imports from the Far East and our closer cousins in France and Germany soon changed the scene. We tried to fight back with such slogans as 'Buy British', but to no avail. The land of the rising Nissan Sunny had come to stay.

At Leisure

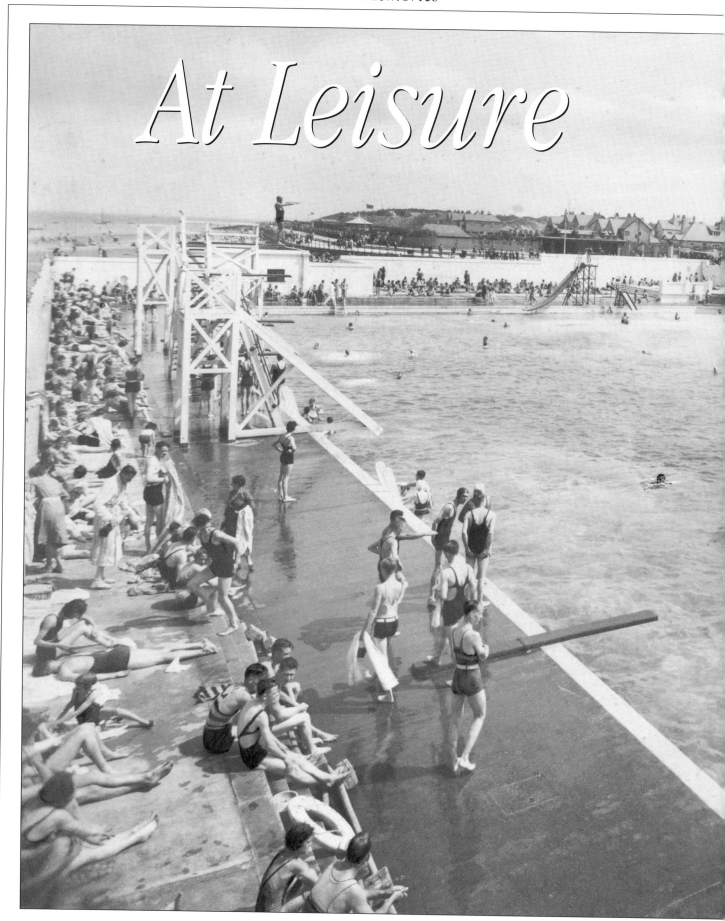

What jolly times were being had at the open air Hoylake swimming pool in 1931. Young beaus tried to emulate the Olympic swimmer and eventual Tarzan, Johnny Weissmuller, as they sought to impress the girls with their aquatic ability. All they got for their pains were a few giggles and some knowing looks. They had to be careful, for mixed bathing was still thought by some to be rather risqué. Just over 20 years earlier the height of women's fashion saw floor length skirts and high necked blouses on Edwardian ladies. They were not about to change their opinions on modest dress, however much the roaring 20s had tried to influence them. When the baths opened in 1913 no mixed bathing was permitted on Tuesdays and Thursdays for part of the day, during which time women had the waters to themselves. Originally, the tide did the job of filling the baths, but this brought in mud, silt and objects too disgusting to describe that hardly made the new attraction as popular as had been initially hoped. Not surprisingly, it was rebuilt in the 1920s at a cost of £25,000, though it was not officially reopened until 1931. After the council closed the baths in 1976 the Hoylake Pool and Community Trust tried to breathe new life into them, but their venture was unsuccessful and the buildings were demolished.

Main picture: All the fun of the fair was there for you on New Brighton's Promenade Pier in the summer of 1941. It was good to escape from the worries of the war and its deprivations. Everybody had a loved one on active service and knew someone who had lost a family member to those horrid hostilities. Not that those on the pier were immune from the dangers because darkness meant that the skies might soon be filled with bomber planes from Hermann Goering's Luftwaffe, hell bent on destroying our industry and our homes. The barrage balloon, or 'blimp' as some called it, that hovered overhead meant that people could not completely switch off from the thought of war, but if they kept their heads down they could pretend for just a while. The helter skelter, Ferris wheel and Octopus rides probably seem tame to modern youth, used to the mighty rollercoasters they ride in the big theme parks, but they were just as popular in their day. The pier opened in September 1867, replacing one that was solely used for access to the ferry. The council bought the pier in 1928, extensively repairing and restoring it before its reopening in 1931.

Inset: In 1933 the country was in the grip of the depression that saw record numbers out of work. The land that Lloyd George had promised would be one fit for heroes after the Great War now seemed a sorry place to be. Mobs rioted on the streets, families went hungry and some men, disillusioned by the attitude of employers and government, turned to the policies of extremists for their salvation. At home, Oswald Mosley's fascist views attracted followers and, in Germany, a little man with a funny moustache became the country's Chancellor. Not that these problems seemed to have been affecting anyone at Egremont. Couples and families were taking the air in a busy, but relaxed atmosphere. A mile along the coast from Seacombe, Egremont Pier was the longest on the Mersey. Its promenade became a popular place for courting couples to stroll and enjoy each other's company as various sweet nothings were whispered away from the hearing and eagle eye of an over protective parent. Egremont shares its name with the small town in Cumbria that was the birthplace of John Askew, the man who developed this area in the 19th century. The pier had been damaged in 1932 when it was hit by an oil tanker, but when a coaster collided with the structure in 1941 the damage was too severe for repairs to be effected. It was eventually scrapped in 1946.

Below: Children are not quite as sophisticated as they or the advertising world would have you believe. Even though there are electronic gadgets galore around them and video games to be played, they still love to use the best playstation of all, the local playground. Whether kicking a ball across its turf or flying high into the sky on its swings, there is something special about a playground. The reason is quite simple. It is for children. Adults do not whiz down slides, bounce up and down on see-saws or spin on roundabouts. These are pursuits for the every young. Arrowe Park, seen in 1960, is just one of countless areas that have such provision, though this one on central Wirral is larger than most. Situated between Thingwall and Woodchurch, it is part of the large 425 acre country park that was originally the estate of John Shaw, a Liverpool warehouse owner. He built Arrowe Hall, now a residential school, in 1835, using local stone, and erected a pair of fine ornamental gates though which the park can be entered. Birkenhead Corporation bought the park for public use in 1928. The youngsters enjoying their day in the great outdoors when this scene was captured will have taken their own offspring here in later years and, more than likely, will be contemplating the same for the grandchildren who are arriving any day now.

Above: Enjoying a day out on New Brighton's sands, this family posed for the camera before taking a traditional ride. It was not a cheap way of passing the time with a group of teenage children who had already been in the funfair and had the regulation bag of chips, but who could begrudge them the chance to hop on the back of Neddy? Could that be your dad in the flares and if so, which of the creatures on show looked more like a donkey? At least the four footed variety had ears as we were never sure whether or not the 70s' generation possessed any. Any young man with an extravagant hairstyle from the early part of that decade will now be in his mid 40s. It is a sure thing that those locks are now carefully trimmed and thinning just a little. How quaint the fashion of yesterday always seems and, yet, how trendy we thought we looked at the time. It does not matter whether it was the cloche hats and flapper dresses of the 1920s, the drainpipe trousers and Edwardian jackets of the 1950s or flowery shirts and platform soles of the 1970s. Whatever the style, how dated it now looks. It will be just the same in about 2030 when we look back at the clothing of today and laugh at young men with shirts outside their trousers and women with pierced belly buttons showing under crop tops.

Wartime

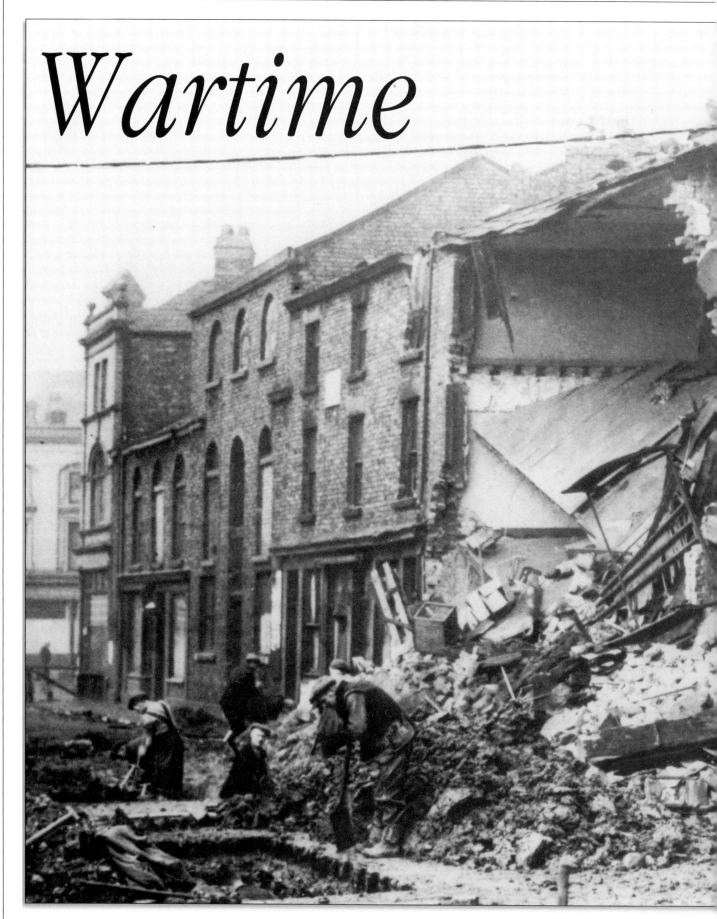

Oh that we never have to live through such times again. This scene of devastation on the lower end of Birkenhead's Grange Road was typical of many others found across the town during the blitzes in 1940 and 1941. Even if no lives were lost, a family returning from the bomb shelter and greeted with such a sight knew that its world had fallen apart. Gone were the memories locked in the rubble of what was not a house, but a home. The postcard from Auntie Flo on the mantelpiece, little Ronnie's teddy bear, the sofa where mum and dad shared their first cuddle and the Christmas crib that our Maureen made at Sunday school meant so much, but were now obliterated. Pity, too, those charged with clearing up the mess. Workmen sifting through the mortar dust, broken beams and shattered brickwork were never sure what they would find. The next movement of the shovel might reveal a severed limb or a burned face. No wonder that they seldom talked about their experiences when they returned home, but the memories of what they discovered brought them nightmares long after the bombs had stopped raining down. Only today's pensioners can recall those days, but the modern generation would do well to reflect that nostalgia for the past only goes so far.

Below: Air Raid Precautions (ARP) were only kicked into life as the inevitability of war dawned on our lords and masters at Whitehall. Yet, the writing on the wall had been plain to see for several years. Fascist forces had been more than flexing their muscles as Italy invaded Abyssinia, Germany annexed neighbouring territories and the Spanish civil war gave us first hand evidence of the terror and havoc that could be wrought from the skies upon defenceless citizens. If ever we needed an example of how defenceless we were in our homes, then the destruction of the historic Basque city of Guernica in the spring of 1937 by German planes that were assisting General Franco's bid for power, brought it home with grim reality. Even so, it would be another year before ARP preparations really began to take shape. Civil defence groups began giving instruction classes on self help in the event of an air raid attack, but it was not until Hitler's invasion of Czechoslovakia in late 1938 that the majority began to take the threat of war seriously. Suddenly, air raid shelters were distributed and sirens sounded the start of practice runs for the emergency services. Volunteers were sought to become wardens and soon became versed in the cry 'Put that light out' that Britons came to hear so often during the blackout when hostilities began in earnest. The men in gas masks on the back of the recruiting lorry remind us of a major fear the population had at the start of the war. The use of aeroplanes as vehicles for releasing bombs that contained mustard gas, phosgene or other agents of chemical warfare was a strong possibility. Fortunately, the enemy was just as apprehensive of a similar retaliatory strike and so a stalemate existed over using this form of attack upon the nation.

Above: Looking typically jaunty, First Lieutenant J Stevens was proud to pose with some of the men from 'Thunderbolt'. Described in despatches as 'a brilliant achievement', they had helped sink an escorted Italian submarine and play their part in bringing the end of the second world war a little nearer. This submarine replaced the ill fated 'Thetis' that sank in Liverpool Bay in June 1939 when undergoing trials. Despite a three day operation by 21 ships of the Royal Navy, more than 70 men remained trapped and eventually drowned after what must have been a horrible and harrowing experience. Just four men escaped before the vessel slipped to the bottom of the sea. Its battered hull was eventually raised and refitted, returning to active duty as 'Thunderbolt' in November 1939. Under the command of Lieutenant Cecil Crouch, everyone on board was a volunteer and knew that she was the old 'Thetis'. On 15 December 1940 she recorded her first 'kill', sinking the Italian 'Tarantini'. Further success came her way, but 'Thunderbolt' became another war casualty on 14 March 1943 when sunk by an Italian sloop. With thoughtless timing, the Admiralty announced the loss on the fourth anniversary of the sinking of the 'Thetis'.

The best side of the law

Sooner or later we could all do with the assistance of a lawyer. Helping folk buy a house, making a will, forming a business partnership, dealing with the consequences of road accidents and divorces are just a selection from the circumstances in which we may find ourselves in need of some legal advice.

One firm of solicitors which has been providing such advice for far longer than most is that of Lees & Partners with offices in Hamilton Square, Birkenhead, Telegraph Road, Heswall and Vicars Lane, Chester. Throughout the course of more than a hundred years the 'Lees Approach' has been a genuine and personal interest in helping clients to resolve their problems: today, as a result, the grandchildren and even great grandchildren of the founder's clients still use the firm.

The firm was founded in 1889 by George Frederick Lees. GF Lees had trained at Reinhart Halsall Solicitors before setting up an office for himself as soon as he was qualified on the first floor of 45 Hamilton Square, Birkenhead.

In those now far off days GF Lees employed just one member of staff: his secretary. Little could he have imagined that by the 21st century the firm he created would have no fewer than ten partners, and employ 16 lawyers and 55 support staff.

The firm eventually expanded to 44 Hamilton Square, and would later occupy part of 43 Hamilton Square as well as its offices in Heswall and Chester.

The founder's eldest son Fred J Lees joined his father after he also had qualified as a solicitor. George Lees however died suddenly in his fifties and FJ Lees invited his youngest brother, George C 'Dubby' Lees to join him as a trainee, subsequently offering him a place in the business on his qualification.

During the second world war FJ Lees and his secretary Maureen Murphy held the firm together. Work was at a minimum during both world wars. After each conflict the firm had to be built up again.

FJ Lees retired in the late 1960s followed by his young brother GC Lees in 1979, by then the next generation was already well established. FJ Lees' daughter Jean

Top: George Frederick Lees, founder of the firm. **Below left:** *44/45 Hamilton Square.* **Below:** *The firm's Heswall offices.*

had joined the firm but had left on marriage: her son however, had worked for the firm in the 1970s and 80s.

GC Lees' son Peter Lees had joined the firm in 1962: he qualified in 1968 and would work for the firm until his own retirement in 2003.

Such long service was not uncommon: Maureen Murphy had been FJ Lees' secretary for half a century, whilst legal executive Ernest Ellam ,who had joined the firm at the age of 16 would stay there all his working life.

When Maureen Murphy had joined the firm the secretary's duties had included lighting the office fire, cooking lunch for FJ Lees, and arranging tea and buns each afternoon. Lees was the first local firm of solici-

tors to get a dictation machine - though it looked like a belt-sander!

GF Lees & Son merged with FS Moore & Price to become Lees Moore & Price in 1983. In 1987 the firm also incorporated Whitley & Co and Edward Lloyd & Co to become Lees Lloyd Whitley. In 1994 however that large grouping demerged and went back to its roots, emerging as Lees & Partners.

Today, private clients and small to medium size business are the firm's main clients. Though the client base is mainly located on the Wirral, that geographical spread is increasing all the time due to recommendations by existing clients and specialisation in certain areas of law. Those clients are impressed by the legal knowledge displayed by the firm, but equally so by its approachable lawyers who work with clients on a personal basis.

In future Lees & Partners aim to build upon its success, and on its fine reputation, both gained by providing quality legal services to the folk of the Wirral for more than century.

Top: Frederick John Lees (left) and George Cecil Lees.
Left: Lees & Partners' Chester offices.
Below left: A group photograph of the Partners, early 2003. Below: Peter Lees, the third generation of the his family to have practised from 44/45 Hamilton Square.

Events & Occasions

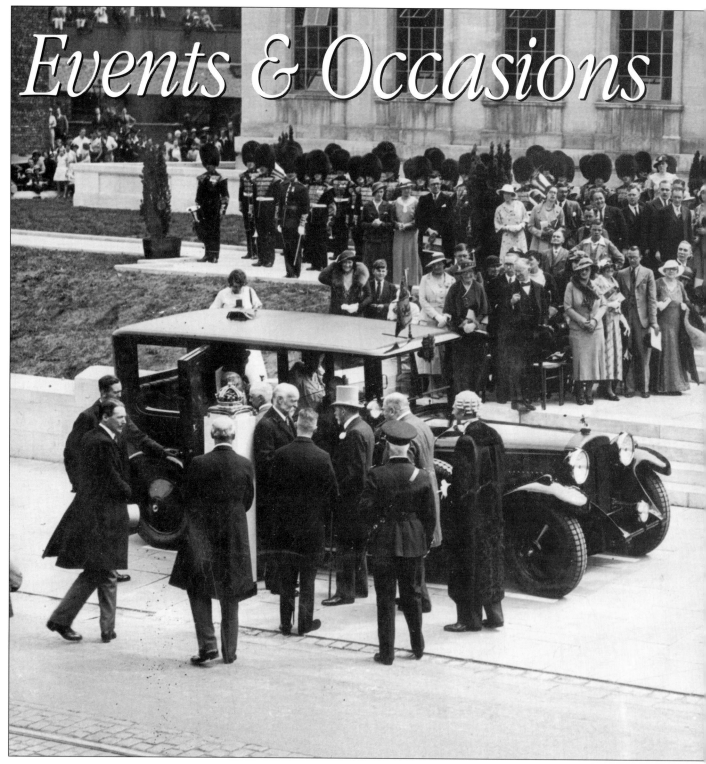

Above: It was only the high and mighty who were allowed close access to their Majesties on 18 July 1934. The bigwigs in their top hats, uniforms, furs and council chains were permitted to be close by, but the ordinary citizens were kept at arm's length. They made do with lining the streets and sitting on rooftops to get a glimpse of the King and Queen who were loved and revered across the land. George V and Queen Mary were a popular couple who had been our figureheads during the dark days of World War I. They were loudly applauded when they abandoned the family name of Saxe Coburg Gotha, with its obvious Germanic connections, in favour or Windsor. Now we actually had a royal family that sounded British. The King further endeared himself to the general public with his frequent expressions of xenophobia and stated dislike of most things foreign. 'Abroad? Been there, didn't like it', is supposed to

Below: It was a proud day for the cadets chosen to greet the royal train and its chief passenger, King George V, when they arrived at Platform 3 in Hooton Station. He was on his way to Port Sunlight to get a first hand view of the model town established by the soap magnates William and James Lever in 1888. The brothers soon instituted other employee benefits, including pensions, medical care, unemployment compensation, profit sharing and free insurance. William was raised to the peerage as Baron Leverhulme in 1917. By 1925 the firm served a world market through a system of 250 associated companies. The dapper monarch would be well pleased with the visit that was part of a programme of meeting his subjects in the months leading up to his 1935 silver jubilee celebrations. The first section of the railway track that brought His Majesty to Hooton opened in 1866 and was extended 20 years later. The service prospered as it linked small agricultural communities as well as opening up the Wirral's resorts to holidaymakers. It was also a boom to the coal workings at Neston Colliery. However, the opening of the 1934 Mersey Tunnel saw business on the line begin to taper off, though it still ran a passenger service until 17 September 1956 and a goods service for a further six years. Coincidentally, the current Lord Leverhulme opened Wirral Country Park, created over the old railway line, in 1973.

have been one of his epithets. Whether or not the comment was true did not matter. His subjects believed it and warmed to him even more. They flocked in their thousands to witness the great man's arrival on Borough Road to open the new Central Library and the cheering and hip-hurrahs could be heard on the other side of the Mersey.

Below: St Stephen's Church Hall was the venue for this Coronation party on 5 June 1953. It took place three days after the real event, but the children were not complaining. They had already had a great street party on the actual day that Queen Elizabeth II was sitting in Westminster Abbey and you could never have too many iced buns and jelly. Mums in their pinnies slaved away for hours providing the goodies and dads did what all dads do; they lent moral support and put a record on the gramophone. Mayor William Short was the guest of honour, seen here cutting the cake. How many sandwich spread sarnies did he get through during the days surrounding the great day, we wonder? He probably swore that he would never look a custard tart in the face again. After the feasting was over the kiddies waited patiently as the trestle tables were put to one side and then set to with a will in the party games that followed. Pass the parcel was carefully engineered by the person operating the turntable, so that the music stopped at just the right time for one of the little ones to win a prize. Musical bumps and chairs, corners and tunnel ball were all great fun to play, even if greedy little Sheila was sick in the middle of it all, having bounced around with seven chocolate cornflake buns inside her.

Right: The Mayoress, Mrs Short, clambered onto the platform that had been hastily erected in the car park of the Ritz. The fur stole she was wearing typified the sort of fashion that the middle classes chose to wear on important and ceremonial occasions. This was in the days long before animal rights had been heard of and the wearing of fox, chinchilla, sable, ermine or mink stated that you had made it in the society pecking order. We should not criticise Mrs Short for her choice of adornment because we would be applying the values of an era half a century removed from her day. Wearing gloves, one of the signs of a true lady, she laid the crown on the head of the festival queen on 2 June 1953 as part of the Coronation celebrations. How proud the recipient must have been. No doubt she still has a copy of a photograph of that special day pasted into her personal album. Whether or not the two little lads by her feet will recall the occasion as fondly is open to debate. They are more likely to cringe with embarrassment as they recall the day when mum scrubbed their faces, combed their hair, made them put on a bow tie and told them that they looked as pretty as a picture.

Above right: Postwar estates and housing developments meant that Upton expanded from the little village that it had been before the builders moved in. However, as a link with those earlier, sleepy days, the main road at its centre is still referred to as 'The Village'. The way of life for established residents of this once little spot changed forever and many bemoaned the arrival of the newcomers, resenting the intrusion. However, this ceremony was not the place in which to demonstrate their reservations about the changes in society. In c1953 the foundation stone for the new St Joseph's RC Church was

laid. The new estates had to have their pubs, shops, libraries, clinics and schools, but there was also a place for spiritual needs to be addressed. Half a century ago we were still a nation where going to church on a Sunday was commonplace. The parish priest was an important figure and one whose word and opinion was respected. Mike Trotter, the altar boy given the responsibility of holding the sacred text from which a reading was being taken, must recall this day with pride. He was in the presence of distinguished company as the service was led by the Bishop of Shrewsbury, John Murphy, later to be the Archbishop of Cardiff. Also in attendance, to the bishop's left, was Canon Percival Rees, the parish priest from Sacred Heart, Moreton.

Below: The photograph is merely dated as being from the 1940s, but it is not too fanciful to suggest that the concert could have been taking place in the summer of 1945 as part of the celebrations that marked the end of the second world war. The array of national flags behind the stage, drawn from the ranks of our allies, and the bunting stretched above the audience suggest that this could have been so. The picture was taken in the Tower Theatre, New Brighton, built as a complement to the steel latticed tower that had been completed in 1900. That rival to Eiffel's famous edifice did not stand the test of time. Its upkeep was badly neglected during the Great War as finances were diverted to the war effort and the tower fell into a terminal state of disrepair. It was demolished in 1921, but the theatre lived on. Many famous entertainers trod its boards, including, in its early days, Lillie Langtry, the Jersey Lily, an actress whose beauty turned a few heads, with the future Edward VII being the most notable. Although the theatre was the setting for highbrow entertainment on occasions, variety nights were the most popular events. A mixed bill of singers, comedians, dancers and speciality acts, such as mind reading, ventriloquism, juggling or dogs that could count, guaranteed a good night out. But all good things come to an end. Television killed off variety halls and the Tower Theatre closed in 1955 and became the large amusement arcade that burned down in 1976.

Right: We know how to party on the Wirral. We did it in 1945 to celebrate VE and VJ Days and repeated the dose in 1953 for the Queen's coronation. But for the fashion styles being worn and the makes of cars in the background, this could have been a scene from any of those previous displays of national joy. But, time had moved on and it was now 6 June 1977 on Charlotte Road, Wallasey. There is nothing much to mark out this side street behind Egremont's King Street, but the kiddies revelled in being the centre of attention for the day. Just like their forebears, these youngsters did not truly appreciate the significance of the day. For them it was a good to have fun and who can begrudge them that? The Queen had been on the throne for 25 years and her silver jubilee was marked across the country by similar street parties. Prophets of doom had forecast that a lack of interest in the monarchy would make the day an anticlimax. How wrong they were as flags flew, sausage rolls were munched and dads played 30 a side soccer in the roadway. Mums and grannies watched all the merriment, thinking back to the other times when the school and church halls were raided for trestle tables and congas were danced in the street to the sound of music played on wind up gramophones.

It was a bright day, with high, fluffy clouds peeking over Wallasey on a summer's morning in c1960. The housewives doing their household shopping went about their business in a very different fashion from the way it would be conducted today. Supermarkets and self service stores were yet to make a major mark and the women moved from butcher to baker and newsagent to grocer, purchasing items and chatting with the shopkeeper at the same time. They paid cash for everything as there were no

Shopping spree

credit cards and many shops did not like to accept cheques. The women were either given their housekeeping from hubby's wage packet or had drawn it out from Martin's Bank, on the right. Getting cash from the teller at the counter is something else that is almost a thing of the past. The hole in the wall has eliminated the need to step through the doors any more and the number of branches that close or become trendy pubs and bars seems to escalate by the minute.

Above: It was obviously wet outside, to judge from the number of raincoats and glistening pacamacs on show. Women's coats were worn at almost ankle length and even those menfolk not noted for their awareness of fashion trends sported theirs down to their calves. However, the number of men on show was not a representative sample as they were few in number and, no doubt, low on interest in the market's china stall. Perhaps those who were in attendance were there to keep a tight rein on the missus' spending. As if she would have taken any notice! A mixture of the wares on sale and the banter of the stallholders attracted the crowd that had gathered. There is a great skill in getting people interested in parting with their money and the mere quality of the goods was not the sole issue. First you had to attract the punters, then keep them entertained and informed and, finally, encourage that parting of the purse strings. Birkenhead's covered

market began life on Market Street on 10 July 1835, but demand was so great that new premises were built on Hamilton Street in 1845. The magnificent 430 feet by 131 feet hall was gutted by fire in 1974 and a major slice of Birkenhead's heritage was lost. A new market was opened in the Grange Precinct in 1977, but still has a link with the old as the original market clock was rescued and ticks away happily in its new home.

Bottom left: Christmas time in the Market Hall and a little tot holding tight to mum's hand seems desperate to reach out to the tree that is just begging to be dragged off to a pride of place in the front room. Plump turkeys wait to be wrapped up and carried away to a hot oven and, in the background, carols can be heard drifting through the dusk. Bright wrapping paper on rolls or in sheets, tinsel, boxes of crackers and paper streamers were a must for a colourful Christmas. We all have fond memories of the preparations that made the festivities perfect for us when we were young. There were the trips to the department store to collect a little present from the grand old white-whiskered man in a red suit. Magic colouring books, tin drums, cherubic dolls and penny whistles were some of the usual treats that Santa had for us. Wasn't it strange that we never commented on how he had lost weight and height when we saw him in a different store no more than an hour later? Back home we put the baubles on the tree that mum had been persuaded

to buy in the market after all. The lights were unwound and, every single year, dad would remark that they were working when he put them away last January. Grandpa dozed by the fire after Christmas lunch as everyone else argued about who could have the battleship token in a family game of Monopoly.

Above: Many of the housewives inside Birkenhead Market in the early 1970s did their shopping bareheaded. A small number wore a hat or headscarf, but the majority did not bother to cover up. How different the scene would have been 20 years earlier. Then it was considered rather lax or even downright common for a lady to be seen out of doors without a head covering of some description. Those days had long gone for most of the shoppers. Anyway, they were far too interested in examining the produce on sale at prices a little cheaper than those asked in the shops or newfangled supermarkets. It was also a good way of ensuring that the apples selected from the fruit counter were just the ones they wanted. They picked up the very specimens that they wished to choose and handed them to the stallholder for weighing. They were not going to fall foul of the sharp practice of some greengrocers who sometimes slipped an overripe or maggoty Cox's pippin into the bag. In the early 1970s the housewife had enough to watch out for in the early days of decimalisation that came their way in February 1971. Out went bobs, florins and half crowns and in came new pence. The shopper lost out, of course, as prices were rounded up and never down, but at least goods were still weighed in pounds and ounces and not the continental mumbo jumbo that has been foisted upon us of late.

Make the most of it, for, in July 1937, this was the last week that the trams would run in Birkenhead. The covered car was a more comfortable affair than some of its predecessors as the first ones had open decks and cabs. Top deck passengers had to brave the elements and drivers came to work with a variety of mufflers, capes and gauntlets to help them get through the worst that the British climate could throw at them. An American, ironically named GF Train, introduced Birkenhead's system in 1860. He was also responsible for bringing the first tramways to London. The town

Transport

was ahead of big city neighbours across the Mersey as Liverpool had to wait five years before its system was started. The noble horse was the main source of power, though some tram companies flirted with steam cars for a while. However, the invention of the dynamo led to the application of transmitted power by means of overhead electrified wires to the trams and, around 1900, the transition took place almost universally. Unfortunately, for our town this was one streetcar that was not named desire and it went to that great depot in the sky a few days after this photograph was taken.

Like some form of confused spaghetti, the railway lines weave in and out of one another and criss-cross in a seemingly random pattern that almost beggars belief that there is some form of systematic organisation at play here. But, it all fitted together and provided a reliable service to the people of West Kirby in 1937. The spur linking the branch to the Wirral line can be seen in the foreground, running off to the joint station platform on the far left. On the far right is the station building that was erected in 1896 and is now the terminus for the Merseyrail Wirral line. When this photograph was taken, the railway was the centre of attraction for land travel. In those great days of steam locomotives, the 1930s brought record speeds on a regular basis for passenger trains. Great names that have gone into the record books and are now permanently etched in our heritage were on the front pages of the national newspapers as the public's imagination was fired up by reports of barriers being broken. In June 1932 the Cheltenham Flyer topped 81 mph, only for the Flying Scotsman to shatter that with 97 mph in 1934. When the London-Newcastle express recorded 108 mph in 1935 everyone thought it incredible, until, that is, the Silver Jubilee and then the Coronation Scot established new records. Pride of place eventually went to the Mallard, which, at 126 mph set in 1938, still holds the steam locomotive record.

Left: The buildings belonging to W Watson and Company on Hamilton Street, Birkenhead later became shop premises, but in 1938 they housed some of vehicles that graced our streets. 'Any colour you like, as long as it's black', as Henry Ford might have said about them, these gleaming examples of the technology of the day now look like some form of Dinky cars, but in their time they were at the sharp end of up to the minute sophistication. Look at the lovely curve of the wheel arches and the practical nature of the running boards. The next time that poor old granny tries to get into your low slung family saloon, and can only do so with the aid of a

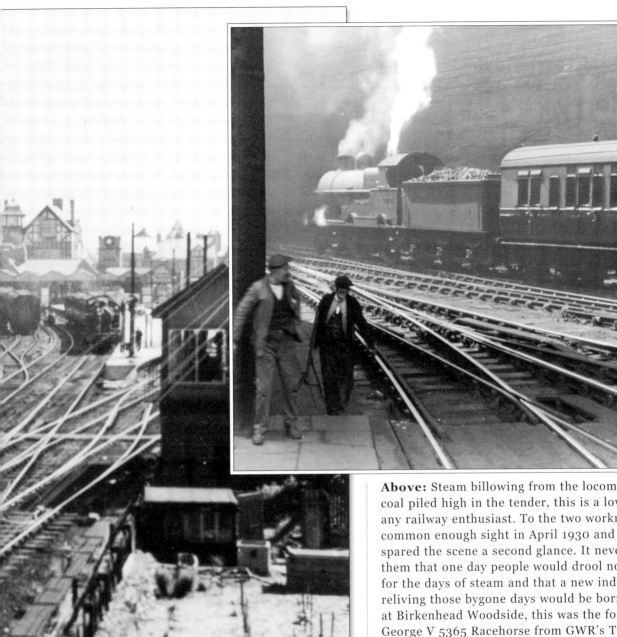

Above: Steam billowing from the locomotive and coal piled high in the tender, this is a lovely sight for any railway enthusiast. To the two workmen it was a common enough sight in April 1930 and they hardly spared the scene a second glance. It never dawned on them that one day people would drool nostalgically for the days of steam and that a new industry of reliving those bygone days would be born. Pictured at Birkenhead Woodside, this was the former LNWR George V 5365 Racehorse from GWR's Toplight stock. The station replaced the one at Monks Ferry when it opened on 1 April 1878 as the terminus of the Chester to Birkenhead line that saw its first trains on 23 September 1840. The Chester and Birkenhead Company amalgamated with Birkenhead, Lancashire and Cheshire Railways in 1847. Woodside was one of a special breed of stations as it serviced trains, trams and ships alike. It closed on 6 November 1967 and became a car park. How we miss the evocative sound of hissing steam and distinctive rumble of such locomotives along the track. The sound even inspired musical acclaim. Close your eyes and imagine the strains of the tune 'Coronation Scot' coming out of the wireless speaker. It must be the theme to the 'Paul Temple' series of detective adventures about to start.

shove as she lurches into place, think how much easier it was for to step into and out of the car back then. Running boards were also very useful for Chicago gangsters to stand on as they emptied their machine gun magazines at one another. Just seeing such cars brings back memories of Robert Stack as crime buster Eliot Ness in the popular 1960s' TV show 'The Untouchables'. Look, too, at the shiny headlights perched on the wings and the side or rear mounted wheel, the latter so much more accessible than today's spare that is tucked away somewhere beneath the shopping in the boot. Lovely old motors, lovely old memories.

Above: What a great sight for steam buffs and monarchists alike. The two became one on 11 July 1957 as the royal train chuffed its way along the track near Kirby Park, originally the small country halt on the Parkgate to West Kirby line that opened in 1894. This section of track had been laid eight years earlier, but most of those in the crowds on the embankment were not too interested in the history of the railway. Although a few had brought notebooks to write down engine numbers and record their sightings, the majority was there to share in the occasion of the Queen's visit to Wallasey. As the dark claret livery of the royal train sped by, the onlookers craned their necks to catch a glimpse of the woman who was but five years into the reign that everyone hoped would be a new Elizabethan age of British glory. There were some hopeful signs and even the staid figure of the prime minister, Harold Macmillan, was moved to declare that 'We had never had it so good' during a speech to a rally he made later that month. There was certainly a feel good factor in the crowd that day as Union flags were waved and cries of 'God bless her' could be heard. Whether or not the same scene and sentiments will be repeated for her eldest son after his accession remains a moot point. Wirral Country Park now extends along the site of the old track.

Below: This spot is close to where the old market once stood on land donated by Francis Price. Photographed in the early 1960s, Market Place South was obviously not the place to be if you wanted to get somewhere in a hurry. How the drivers must have been fretting and fuming as they sat in this long tailback and how we can sympathise with their plight as we do just the same thing ourselves on numerous streets today. It made little difference if you were riding in a baby Austin or a sleek Jaguar. Zero miles per hour was the great leveller. The French have a saying about la plus ça change... and how right they are. The exhaust fumes on Market Place South must have had a high toxic reading because catalytic converters and emission controls were for the future. At least we did not have to contend with the smog from which we had suffered a decade before. Gases from car exhausts were a contributory factor, but industrial and domestic chimneys were the main causes of that dirty, health threatening pall that shrouded us and covered our clothing with grime every winter. A succession of Clean Air Acts in the early 1950s made smog a thing of the past. What a pity the powers that be cannot legislate properly to cure congestion on the streets as they did for our lungs.

Below: Anyone in an anorak shed a tear that dampened his exercise book, causing the ink of thousands of carefully recorded train numbers to run down the pages. The railway came to Hoylake in 1866, linking it to the Docks station at Birkenhead. An extension to West Kirby was undertaken in 1879 and businessmen and merchants bought property in the more rural areas of the Wirral, knowing that they could commute to their places of work. The railway helped townships to grow and brought greater prosperity to the area and its coast, and helping to open it up to holidaymakers and day trippers who had money burning holes in their pockets. But, the great days of rail were over at 'the joint' at West Kirby. It was the same across the country with small stations and branch lines closing as they were deemed uneconomic. Sacrificed on the altar of the great god of progress, its high priest Dr Beeching ordered the closure of large chunks of our network, much to the disgust of traditionalists and travellers alike. On 7 May 1962 the last freight train, headed by a LMS 2-6-4 tank engine (no 42229), left on its final journey to Hooton. Even youngsters not noted for their sense of history knew that something sad was afoot, as can be seen by their body language as they mournfully waved goodbye, not just to a train, but to an era of our transport history.

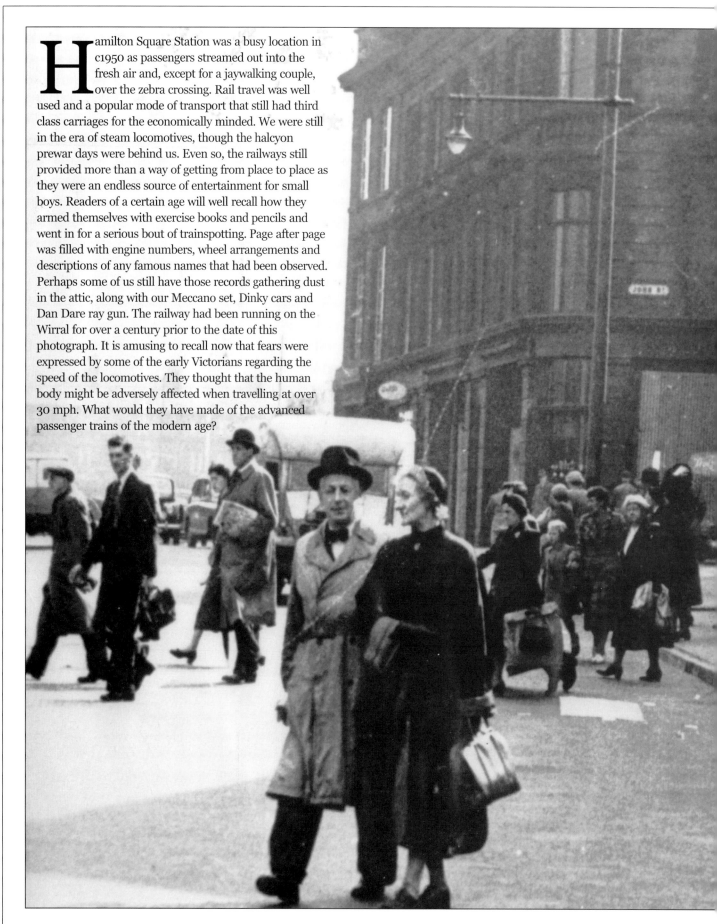

Hamilton Square Station was a busy location in c1950 as passengers streamed out into the fresh air and, except for a jaywalking couple, over the zebra crossing. Rail travel was well used and a popular mode of transport that still had third class carriages for the economically minded. We were still in the era of steam locomotives, though the halcyon prewar days were behind us. Even so, the railways still provided more than a way of getting from place to place as they were an endless source of entertainment for small boys. Readers of a certain age will well recall how they armed themselves with exercise books and pencils and went in for a serious bout of trainspotting. Page after page was filled with engine numbers, wheel arrangements and descriptions of any famous names that had been observed. Perhaps some of us still have those records gathering dust in the attic, along with our Meccano set, Dinky cars and Dan Dare ray gun. The railway had been running on the Wirral for over a century prior to the date of this photograph. It is amusing to recall now that fears were expressed by some of the early Victorians regarding the speed of the locomotives. They thought that the human body might be adversely affected when travelling at over 30 mph. What would they have made of the advanced passenger trains of the modern age?

Above: The 'Thunderbird' was a handbuilt Merryweather fire engine, delivered to the Birkenhead fire brigade in 1952. This fine machine was one of only three of its type ever produced. The chairman of the Watch Committee and the Chief Fire Officer stood proudly alongside the handsome vehicle that looks rather quaint over half a century later, but at the time it was the bees' knees of firefighting. Merryweather had a long association with the fire service. Merryweather and Sons was originally established around 1690 by a Nathaniel Hadley whose London factory manufactured, among other things, pumps and fire-fighting apparatus. The first fire engine factory was built in 1738 and was used to make hand engines and leather hose, and later for steam engines. In 1791 the firm and became Hadley, Simpkin and Lott before passing into the hands of Moses Merryweather, who had apprenticed there in 1807, and his three sons. As 'Fire Engine Makers by Appointment to His Majesty the King', Merryweather and Sons sold fire-fighting apparatus to cities around the world. By 1913 its machines were being used across the UK, in South Africa, Australia, India and China. It went from strength to strength in the interwar years as the company name became synonymous with quality fire engines, but the only modern production machines now found come as Matchbox replica toys.

The bobby on point duty seems to be throwing up his hands in despair as though he is resigned to the fact that the traffic near Central Station is running out of control. Those white gloved hands, waving just as dramatically as any conductor wielding a baton, have been blessed with awesome power. With just one imperious movement he can halt a whole stream of traffic. Unfortunately, the sheer volume of cars, bikes, buses and lorries on our streets in the 1950s could achieve that all on their own. Getting it all to move smoothly was more difficult to achieve. The postwar boom in car ownership began in the mid 1950s and, within a few years, what had once

been the mark of the wealthy middle classes was becoming more of a norm for everyone. Cheaper family saloons and the widespread availability of hire purchase helped even the humblest of families aspire to owning their own car. Most of the models were British, of course, but there was one popular interloper from abroad. The Volkswagen Beetle, despite its origin in the land of our recent deadly enemy, had few rivals in its class until Issigonis designed Britain's version of the 'people's car', the BMC Mini. Mopeds, sidecars and motorbikes were popular modes of transport, but many of these riders would soon increase the number of their wheels to four.

As an island race we have always appreciated the value of our shipping and the importance it had in putting the 'great' into Great Britain. During the Victorian era, when we were truly a mighty nation, it is no coincidence that our great ships ensured that dominance in trade and influence on the world stage. Birkenhead played its part in the great scheme of things. The community was a hamlet of 106 inhabitants as late as 1810. Its subsequent rapid development began with the establishment of boiler works and a shipyard on Wallasey Pool, a creek of the Mersey, in 1824. In 1828 proposals were made for the conversion of Wallasey Pool into an artificial basin. The first docks were built in less than five years and opened in 1847. This photograph shows Alfred Dock and the dock entrance gates, with Tower Road and Pump Road to the bottom and Seacombe and its ferry terminal towards the top, just below where the entrance to the Kingsway Tunnel now stands. Besides sharing in the general trade of the Mersey, Birkenhead developed an individual trade in the export of manufactures from the midlands, the import of cattle from Ireland and the export and import of goods with the eastern tropics. Although shipbuilding and associated engineering declined dramatically in the second half of the last century, the dockland area now thrives with new commercial developments.

At the Docks

This aerial view of the Great Floats was taken looking from above Alfred Dock and across the Bascule Bridge. Vittoria Dock is centre left, with Duke Street Bridge beyond. The important flour mills are to the top right and Seacombe's Dock Road hugs the right hand side of the photograph. Shipbuilding was one of the mainstays of the local economy and Birkenhead can boast many firsts in its naval history. The world's first iron steamship, 'John Randolph', was built here but one of the most moving histories is attached to a ship that bore the town's name. The 'Birkenhead' was a frigate that became a byname in naval courage and steadfastness. The frigate was acting as a troopship when it foundered in 1852 off the coast of Capetown. The only serviceable lifeboat was given over to the small contingent of women and children on board and, as the little craft left with its precious cargo, some 600 servicemen stood stoically to attention, knowing the fate that awaited them. The vast majority drowned, but their memory lives on in the annals of heroism on the high seas. The story of the docks at Birkenhead began in 1828, but there can never have been a true life story as noble as the one told about the men of the 'Birkenhead'.

In 1937 the spacious promenade deck of the new 'Mauretania' was taking shape at Cammell Laird's yard. Some of the largest craft afloat were built here, especially around the turn into the 20th century. In the 1920s it turned out the first ever all welded ship and, during the second world war, built such fighting mammoths as the 'Ark Royal', 'Prince of Wales' and 'Achilles'. The 'Mauretania' would see active service during that period when she was converted to a troopship in March 1940 and used initially on the Australia to Suez run. Later she served by transporting American soldiers to Europe. The 35,739 ton Cunard liner was 232 metres in length and ran at a speed of 23 knots. She was commissioned as a form of active reserve ship to back up the London sailings of the 'Britannic' and 'Georgic', as well as relieving the pressure on business whenever the two 'Queens' were out of service for overhauling. Until the launching of 'Windsor Castle' in 1959, the 'Mauretania' was the largest liner built on Merseyside. She returned to passenger service in 1946 and was fitted out with air conditioning in 1957. Further remodelling took place in 1962, but she was only to last a further three years before being consigned to the breaker's yard.

On 28 July 1938 the 'Mauretania' gracefully slid down the slipway from the Cammell Laird yard into the river ready to start a life of varied service. The occasion was watched by a packed crowd of whom many had been directly involved in the construction of the latest example of expert British engineering to come out of the world famous shipyard. The liner bore a famous name. Nicknamed 'The grand old lady', the original 'Mauretania' was launched in 1906, making its maiden voyage the following year. It held the Blue Riband for the fastest Atlantic crossing until 1929 and made 269 double journeys across the big pond before being taken out of service in 1934 and scrapped a year later. The second 'Mauretania', part of the Cunard White Star Line, was classed as an intermediate North Atlantic liner and was designed as a compromise between the super liners of the day and smaller vessels. She combined large liner luxury with slower speed and an increased capacity for cargo handling. This ship was not as sleek as her predecessor, but her 1,169 passengers travelled in greater comfort. The 'Mauretania' left Southampton on her final voyage to New York on 4 August 1965. After cruising the Mediterranean she was sailed to the Firth of Forth on 23 November 1965 and scrapped at Inverkeithing.

Bird's eye view

Below: Birkenhead's Hamilton Square is not at the geographic centre of the town, but it is the spot from where the rest seems to radiate. Many of the handsome buildings on the perimeter were made from Storeton stone and their lofty presence mark the importance of the square in local history. The town hall, on its south side, is very similar to Bolton Town Hall, a building that dates from the same mid Victorian era, though our centre of local administration was opened in 1887, some 14 years after its close cousin. It was fitting that John and William Laird, the grandsons of the man who had founded Hamilton Square in honour of his wife's family name, were called upon to perform the opening ceremony of Birkenhead Town Hall. Since local government reorganisation in 1974 the building ceased to function in its original capacity and now is home to the Wirral Museum. Looking across Hamilton Square towards the dockland, the gardens and lawns present a delightful picture of green tranquility that is the envy of larger cities that have little to equal them. Birkenhead was a true Victorian boom town, but at least the planners had the foresight to preserve some of England's green and pleasant land within its heart.

Below: In 1968 the approach roads to the new Mersey tunnel were taking shape. The river had been crossed centuries before when Benedictine monks founded the ferry close to their priory, but another form of transport ploughed a new route from one side to the other when the railway tunnel was built in 1886. Even though there were a number of ferry services operating in addition to the rail link, the advent of the motor car and the rapid growth in population on Merseyside meant that the established passenger services were stretched to the limit. The problem became particularly acute after World War I and outline plans were drawn up to build a bridge across the river. Certain council members poured cold water on this idea, fearing it could be a focal point for enemy action if war broke out again. Eventually the idea was rejected in favour of a road tunnel and work was begun in 1925. Its ventilation shafts rose 200 feet into the air, but these blots on the landscape were a small price to pay for the convenience the tunnel offered. Tunnelling from both banks, the historic joining up of the two segments took place in 1928 and the respective mayors of Liverpool and Birkenhead ceremonially greeted each other far below the river. King George V performed the official opening ceremony of the Queensway Tunnel in 1934. By the 1960s it was obvious that the tunnel could not cope with the volume of traffic that abounded. The first tube of the new Kingsway Tunnel was opened three years after this photograph was taken, with the full project being completed in 1973.

At work

This 1920s' police and tradesmen's outing was about to set off in the finest charabancs that Harding's could provide. Let us hope that the weather stayed fine for them in the open tourers. History does not relate their destination; perhaps it was to a North Wales resort or a mystery tour of the Cheshire countryside. Wherever they were going, the occasion had demanded that they dress properly for the day. Best suits and buttonholes, smart dresses and hats were brought out of wardrobes for the trip. Even though fashions have changed and 'charas' become more luxurious, this sort of scene was being repeated over and over again in the intervening years. However, the height of popularity for the day trip took place either side of the second world war when private car ownership was not widespread. A visit to the seaside would be arranged for a whole street or works' department, so that most of those on board knew one another. The short run to Blackpool or Rhyl was anticipated with great excitement for days beforehand. After enjoyable hours in a deckchair, or strolling along the prom in a 'kiss me quick' hat, the trippers piled back on board their transport. A short stop at a pub or fish and chip shop on the way home topped off the day and, having passed the hat round for the driver, a cheery coach load wished one another good night before going home refreshed and ready for another boring day at work.

Below: The female army of machinists at the CWS Slumberwear factory at Belmont laboured away at their task of pulling material through, stitching, pulling more through and stitching again. It was repetitive by its nature, but for a skilled operative on piece work it had its rewards come pay day. The women built up a sense of camaraderie as they toiled away and many friendships forged here were continued long after the knocking off whistle sounded. There was not a lot of scope for chat while the sewing machines clattered away and, in any case, it was important to concentrate. If the supervisor rejected a piece of work, then that was time spent for no financial return. Additionally, there was the chance of spearing a finger if your mind was not on the job. Light relief was sometimes gained from listening to 'Workers' Playtime' being relayed from the radio. Cheerful Charlie Chester or Big-Hearted Arthur Askey usually had a few gags to make you chuckle, though the one they really liked was often too racy to be given a free rein on the Light Programme. That cheeky chappie, Max Miller, was the one the girls loved. When they saw him in the variety halls they pretended to be shocked when he announced that his next jokes were coming out of his blue book. Shocked or not, they remembered them and repeated them to their workmates at the next morning's tea break.

Right: There is something so satisfying about the feel of a real book that no glossy magazine or data on a CD-ROM can possibly hope to match. The librarians in Birkenhead's new Central Library on Borough Road must have thought that they were in heaven. Row upon row of information and escapism was there at their fingertips. In 1934 they had the opportunity to be at one with the work of new authors who had recently become popular. Although they still cherished the work of beloved 19th century writers, the charm of Jane Austen, the passion of the Brontes, the power of Dickens and the excitement of Conan Doyle, there were now others who could stake a claim to an important place on the shelves. Graham Greene's 'Stamboul Train' was an exciting thriller and there were the involved plots and red herrings of Agatha Christie's whodunits. The earthy novels written by DH Lawrence were now beginning to see the light of day in public libraries, but care had to be taken when handling one of those in case steam poured out of the book's spine. In the days before we became a nation of couch potatoes in front of a TV set, curling up with a good book was the best way of forgetting the world outside and escaping into one brought to life by the art of the story teller.

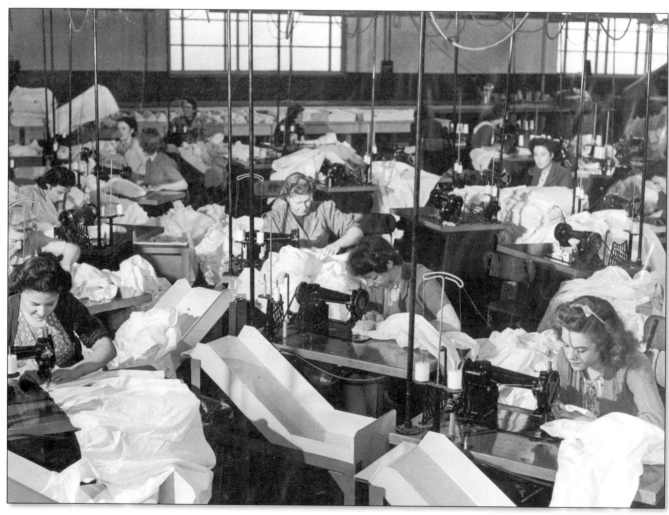

What was going through the mind of the Crosville employee standing in front of the weighing machine outside the bus station at Heswall in 1952? He worked for the company, developed from an electrical machinery firm established by George Crosland Taylor (1857-1923) in 1882, that was to become one of Britain's largest operators and is now part of the National Bus Company. As the man stood, lost in his own thoughts, he might have turned his attention to some of the year's important events. He had a new monarch to serve as Queen Elizabeth II had succeeded her father, George VI, in February. Perhaps this was to be the start of a new Elizabethan era that would lift Britain out of the austerity of the postwar years and into a golden age in the second half of the century. The troubles of recent times were still fresh in his mind and heightened when he read the newly published 'Diary of Anne Frank' that recounted the horrors she and her family endured. However, there was not much in the current news to cheer him up. Widespread flooding hit the west country, drowning 36 in the little Devon resort of Lynmouth, and 112 died in a train crash at Harrow and Wealdstone. With war raging in Korea and Britain successfully testing an atomic bomb, his hopes lay more with a flutter on Vernon's Pools. Perhaps Saturday would bring him eight draws and his future would be secured.

Above: It used to be said that whatever you did at school did not really matter as there was always a job at the shipyards waiting for you. In 1955, this posse of workers streaming out of Cammel Laird's bore witness to that tenet, though they did not realise that those days would not last forever. They looked a happy band of men, perhaps because the hooter had just sounded for the end of the shift and they were off home for their evening meal and a quiet pint or two down at the club. It wasn't always smiles. During this decade industrial relations were not at their best and a series of disputes led to union action. Come the spring, when someone remarked that the daffodils were out he was told that the shipyard workers would soon follow suit. From the evidence in our picture it is obvious that men dominated the working environment. Only a handful of women can be picked out and they would have come from the offices where they acted as tea ladies, typists and clerks. The heavy work was left to the males, even though the opposite sex was deemed fit enough to be pressed into service as fitters and engineers in the war years. It had not taken long for a return to stereotyping on the shop floor and at the dockside.

Centre: This photograph predates even 'Heartbeat', the popular ITV series of recent years about bobbying in the swinging 60s. A somewhat Heath Robinson affair of stretched and tangled cables, this nerve centre of police operations would have the health and safety brigade turning purple with rage at the sight of knotted wiring and connectors dangling in space just waiting to short out and fry some unfortunate operative sitting beneath. This was in the days when the friendly bobby was a reality and one could be seen ambling along the pavement, ever ready to lend a hand to a distressed soul without the need to first pin him to the wall with legs astride as a vanload of others in body armour piled out of a van. The policeman now on the beat can also bemoan his lot because, to earlier generations, it seemed fair enough for a real villain to get a thump or a cheeky brat a clip round the ear without running off to get support from some civil liberties organisation. Today's sergeant at his desk does not take down the details of a reported misdemeanour into a ledger, as this chap was doing, but will rely on a civilian keying data into a computer and then giving the caller a crime number. In our picture the information was acted upon and a victim got personal service as an appropriate Dixon of Dock Green type was sent, bicycle clips at the ready, to your door. 'Evenin' all'.

Bottom: Many old school buildings have, carved into the archways above their entrances, lettering denoting that boys are admitted through one doorway and girls through another. There was no need of any such distinction over the gates at this school, for the segregation by sex was complete. This one was just for boys. Woodchurch Secondary School, Carr Bridge Road, admitted its first pupil on 31 March 1960. It was built on one of the comparatively new housing estates that appeared after the war. There had been an urgent need for new homes since building programmes had been put on hold during the war years and enemy action had destroyed thousands of houses. The new estates were like mini villages, usually with their own small shopping centres, clinics, pubs and schools. In the main, the children attending Woodchurch Boys' School did not have far to travel. They found the surroundings much more light and airy than the older buildings from where they had transferred. The teacher in this classroom was obviously a modern thinker, with charts and informative posters on the wall, though there was no sign of the students' work on display. The fad for double mounting their written efforts and straight pinning them on to stands covered with black sugar paper was a decade away. The school is now part of Woodchurch High, situated close to Junction 3 of the M53 motorway.

20,000 days under the sea

In 2003 the British Sub Aqua Club, whose headquarters today are at Telford Quay, Ellesmere Port, celebrated its 50th anniversary.

The club was born a mere ten years after the French aqualung inventor, Jacques Cousteau, had made his first pioneering dives.

Entrepreneur Oscar Gugen and a young journalist Peter Small had visited Britain's first diving school, run by former RAF test pilot Trevor Hampton in Dartmouth in Devon, in the Autumn of 1953. They were so enthralled they determined to form a new club for like-minded folk.

Small and Gugen returned to London and on 15th October 1953 held a meeting at the Waldorf Hotel Aldwych, London, attended by 100 fellow divers at which they formed the British Sub-Aqua Club.

Such was the BSAC's status that by 1960 the Duke of Edinburgh had agreed to become the club's president.

Two years later the BSAC hosted a congress for the 'World Underwater Federation' an event which featured Jacques Cousteau himself as its guest speaker. Cousteau astonished delegates by proposing that one day gills might be grafted onto humans creating 'Homo Aquaticus'.

The 1960s would be a fascinating decade for the BSAC. Southsea members of

the BSAC John Towse and Alexander McKee discovered the wreck of the now-famed Mary Rose after spotting an obscure mark on a hydrographic chart. The pair made the first historic dive to the Tudor warship on 14th May 1966 in zero visibility, but it would take four more years before the wreck could be formally identified.

The following year Operation Kelp was a massive environmental project organised by the not-yet-famous David Bellamy. The project involved 25 BSAC branches and no fewer than 262 members. Members were recruited to take kelp samples from the North Sea to check on pollution levels. Bellamy and the divers involved received the Duke of Edinburgh Prize for their hard work, whilst David Bellamy became the Club's Science Officer.

Top: Jacques Cousteau (seated) as guest speaker at a congress for the World Underwater Federation, 1962. Below left: Entrepreneur Oscar Gugen. Left: HRH The Duke of Edinburgh, first president of the BSAC. Below: The wreckage of the Mary Rose discovered by BSAC Southsea members John Towse and Alexander McKee.

Alex Flinder became BSAC chairman in 1969 and was influential in facilitating the use of amateur divers in marine archaeology and in the promotion of the Wreck Protection Act.

That same year Dr Colon Martin oversaw a major expedition off the coast of Ireland which resulted in the location of the wreck of the Santa Maria de la Rosa, a long lost Spanish galleon.

In 1970 BSAC divers John Bevan and Peter Sharphouse spent ten hours submerged in a chamber 1,500 ft (492m) below the surface of the sea. The dive, which also involved a total of 12 days inside the Navy chamber at Gosport in Hampshire, disproved the then current theory that divers would experience a 'helium barrier' at 1,200 ft which would prevent them from ever venturing deeper.

By the time of BSAC"s 21st birthday in 1974 the club had become a national institution. The celebrations took place at London's Guildhall and were attended by its new president, the Prince of Wales, and comedian, the late Sir Harry Secombe. Few of those present would ever forget Secombe's comic rendition of 'I'm forever blowing bubbles'. Both guests would go on attend the 40th anniversary celebrations in 1993 which also took place at the Guildhall.

The Mary Rose was finally raised in October 1982 - an event watched by an incredible 60 million viewers, until then the BBC's largest ever outside broadcast. BSAC divers from Southsea, Southampton, Brighton and the Isle of Wight, amongst other branches, had worked hard to realise that dream. The Mary Rose Trust's archaeologists and chief divers were all trained by the BSAC. In the final 12 months of the Mary's Rose's life under the waves an astonishing 5,000 dives were made. In total 14,000 artefacts would be recovered from the seabed.

During the 1980s diving would become increasingly popular. The early 1990s saw the introduction of BSAC's 'Learn to Dive' campaign which would see thousands of people given try-dives. The campaign has been repeated every September since then.

The BSAC celebrated its Golden Jubilee in 2003. The anniversary was marked with a whole year of expeditions, branch activities and mass dive-ins. Celebrations would culminate in an historic return to the Waldorf Hotel where the British Sub-Aqua Club story began back in 1953 - getting on for 20,000 days under the sea!

Top left: Dr David Bellamy.
Top centre: NASA Astronaut, Mike Gernhardt, a guest speaker at the BSAC's conference 'Underwater World' at Harrogate in 1998, talking about decompression in Space! Top right: The launch of the BSAC's 'Learn to Dive' campaign in 1995 saw thousands try diving for the first time. Centre: The BSAC's Headoffice at Telfords Quay, Ellesmere Port. Left: TV celebrity Lloyd Grossman (right) pictured with Andrew Miller (left) and Howard Painter (BSAC Chairman 1993-1995) in the Try-Dive Pool at Olympia as part of the BSAC's nationwide 'Learn to Dive' campaign, 1995.

Shop like an Egyptian

It's funny how time flies. The older one gets the faster it seems to go. Buildings, which older readers saw being built have, for a younger generation, always been there - and when we stop to count the passing years we realise with a shock that what we persist in calling 'new' has been around for ten or twenty years. The truth is that history is being created all around us as we watch. That is especially true when it comes to going to the shops.

Though pyramid selling may have got itself a bad reputation in the 1980s Pyramids shopping certainly did not - as the folk of Birkenhead can readily testify.

The Pyramids Shopping Centre began construction in 1986 and was expected to take two years to build. The doors actually opened to the public on 25th August 1989, after the building was formally opened by Henry E Cotton JP the Lord Lieutenant of Merseyside. The opening was nearly 12 months later than planned, completion having been delayed by an unexpected shortage of bricks and glass.

Erected by Sibec Developments Ltd, the new shopping centre had spent much of the building period labelled simply with the uninspiring name of 'Grange 2'. The name 'the Pyramids' began life simply as a local nickname when part of the building's steel frame was seen to have that shape. The building of course bears no serious resemblance to either Egyptian or Aztec pyramids - although since it officially acquired the name everything has been done to capitalise on the unexpectedly acquired fame.

The idea for the shopping centre had been floating around for many years. Plans were actually drawn up soon after the end of the second world war for rebuilding war-damaged Birkenhead to include a covered shopping precinct. Not until the early 1970s did the construction of the Grange Precinct finally take place.

In the early 1980s however the planners' complete dream finally became reality as plans were put together to build the totally covered shopping centre which later would become the Pyramids Shopping Centre. When completed, the glass and brick construction in an imaginatively designed scheme would provide no less than 160,000 sq ft of prime shopping space for famous retailers such as Next alongside many other well known high street names and include an extension to Marks and Spencers.

Linking with the Grange and the town's covered market the Pyramids development created a shoppers' paradise. A major feature of the new centre was its glass lift and escalator entrance, whilst a new 750-space car park was linked to it via a glass-walled pedestrian bridge.

The Pyramids Centre is built on the banks of what was once Birkenhead's 'Happy Valley', the ancient walk known for its happy atmosphere. In 1989 that history,

Top: A model of the Pyramids Shopping Centre.
Below left and below: *Construction of the Pyramids Centre begins.*

unsurprisingly, prompted the developers and others to express the hope that shoppers and visitors to the new centre would also find happiness within its precincts. In fact the whole site has a very long history: Grange Road, for example, lay along an old track used by monks in the 12th century which lead from their priory to their grange. Borough Road follows the wooded route of Happy Valley, but it was not until the 1830s,

when Birkenhead began to grow, that a market first opened there. By the 1870s the town was spreading out from Hamilton Square to Grange Lane - now Grange Road - and shops and stores began appearing in large numbers at the Charring Cross end of the borough, turning it into the town's main shopping area.

Since its opening the Pyramids Shopping Centre has done much to ensure that a continuing flow of shoppers continues to be drawn to it and the area - not least in its first year of opening when the still-unretired champion boxer Frank Bruno visited the centre, followed two months later by a spectacular fireworks display during the course of which Santa Claus arrived by hot air balloon. Since its opening a regular programme of attractions has been laid on by the management to ensure that visitors remain attracted to the centre and can be assured of an all round shopping experience in surroundings which would astonish previous generations.

Left: Commemorating the laying of the foundation stone.
Below: A birds eye view of the Pyramids Shopping Centre and inset, the entrance to the Centre.

Viva Vauxhall

Back in 2002 Vauxhall Motors at Ellesmere Port celebrated four decades of production at its Wirral plant. That event coincided with the 10th anniversary of General Motors' V6 engine facility on the site. But it was in 2003 that Vauxhall could really throw a party: that year the company celebrated its centenary as a car manufacturer, its first horseless carriage having left the original Vauxhall factory in 1903.

The name Vauxhall has its roots in ancient British history. It is derived from an adventurous Plantaganet mercenary soldier called Fulk le Breant, a man who was allegedly hired by the unpopular King John (1166-1216) to perform some of his dirtier military deeds.

For his trouble Fulk was made Sheriff of Oxford and Hertford and granted the Manor of Luton - a Luton connection even then - by a grateful king.

Through his marriage to a wealthy young widow, Margaret de Redvers, Fulk acquired a house on the south bank of the Thames, a building which consequently became known as Fulk's Hall, a name corrupted over the years to Fawkes Hall, Foxhall and ultimately to Vauxhall.

During his climb up the social ladder Fulk was also given the right to his own coat of arms. He chose the mythical griffin - subsequently to become the logo of Vauxhall Motors - as his heraldic emblem, and this was how the Griffin became associated with Luton as early as the 13th century. It would take more than seven hundred years however for the Griffin to find its way north to the Wirral.

Vauxhall had announced plans to build a new £60 million factory at Ellesmere Port on 5th February 1960: components, gearbox assemblies for the F type Victor began rolling off the production line in November 1962.

Above: One of Vauxhall's first cars, a 4-seater 'Standard'. **Top right:** The famous Vauxhall Griffin. **Below:** Engineer Laurence Pomperoy behind the wheel of a Prince Henry prototype, circa 1911.

The location had been decided upon by Vauxhall Directors after visits to many other alternative sites. In common with other leading British motor manufacturers who were undertaking expansion moves at the time, Vauxhall was encouraged by the Government to look for a site in a development area. Among the many locations considered by the company's Directors the disused wartime airfield at Hooton Park appealed for a number of reasons, not least that is was at the centre of good communications by road, rail, air and sea.

The site , varying from 44 to 75 feet above sea level, enabled the main contractors to start building works with a minimum of earth moving.

The first sod was cut on the site in August 1960 but, despite its relative flatness, most of the following year was spent in site preparation and levelling. During 1962 construction began in earnest as services to the site were

put in place, allowing EA block and the Power House to take shape. The Foundation Stone - adjacent to the foyer in EA block - was laid by Dr Charles Hill MP on 22nd November 1962.

The first vehicle, an HA Viva, was produced at Ellesmere Port on 1st June 1964, and through the 1960s and 1970s the factory was responsible for building successive Viva models.

In 1975 the product range was extended to include the Chevette in hatchback, saloon and estate variants.

With the launch of the front wheel-drive Astra in November 1981 Ellesmere Port became 'Home to the Astra'.

In the Autumn of 1984 a £65 million investment programme in new manufacturing methods, sophisticated robotics and other high technology equipment heralded the second generation Astra.

The culmination, in October 1991, of a three year £200 million investment programme brought another new model Astra into production. By the following year Astra sales were up almost 20 per cent with exports accounting for over a third of the total.

Top: *Vauxhall's first factory at Luton pictured in 1905.* **Above left:** *The D-type 25 hp staff car transporting the then prince of Wales and Lord Plumer into Valletta, Malta.*
Right: *The handsome 1930 Hurlingham Tourer, built on a T-type, was the last of Vauxhall's exclusive vehicles, Vauxhall were now to appeal the mass market.*

grown from 200 in 1962 to 4,500 by 1992 making it the Wirral's, indeed Cheshire's, largest private employer.

The Vauxhall story, however, did not begin in Ellesmere Port in the early 1960s. Like so many other famous motoring marques Vauxhall can also trace its origins to a company which began life making products of a very different kind.

In the 17th century pleasure gardens known as the Vaux Hall Gardens were laid out on the site of Fulk le Breant's estate. They reached the zenith of their popularity in the early 19th century before falling into disrepute. The Vauxhall pleasure gardens closed in 1859, two years after one Alexander Wilson had set up his nearby Vauxhall Iron Works. Wilson borrowed Fulk le Breant's heraldic griffin as the emblem of his new business. Alexander Wilson's Vauxhall Iron Works produced marine engines as well as pumps, cranes and other engineering products.

Meanwhile that previously mentioned £190 million General Motors V6 engine facility was on the drawing board to build advanced V6 engines for GM products in Europe. Occupying 37,000 square metres the new facility went on to produce 135,000 engines a year and employing 450 people at full capacity .

By 1992 over two million cars and light vehicles had been produced at Ellesmere Port. The plant's labour force had

Top left: One of the first Bedfords, a standard factory 2-tonner, the shorter WHG model at work in the Rhondda Valley. Top right: The Cresta run - E types roll off the production line at Luton, 1950s. Above: In 1948 the first new post-war models arrived one was this L-type 2.25 litre 6 cylinder Velox. Below: The proposed site for the construction of Vauxhall new plant at Ellesmere Port.
Above right and right: Construction of the Ellesmere Port plant.

It was not until 1903 that the firm first turned its hand to the still novel horseless carriage. By then, however, the founder Alexander Wilson had left the company and it was

through the efforts of FW Hodges, a Wilson-trained marine engineer, and JH Chambers, that the first ever Vauxhall car was built.

That very first Vauxhall car, a 5 horse power model, had just one horizontal cylinder. There was a foot-operated governor on the exhaust valve, a throttle control on the tiller steering arm, just two forward gears - and no reverse. The standard 1903 model, priced at £136, was two-seater. A four seat version was also offered and out of the seventy or so that were manufactured, only two examples survive today.

Problems with the lease of the South London factory prompted the Vauxhall Iron Works to move to Luton in 1905.

Vauxhall's coming of age was in 1907 when a new firm was created - Vauxhall Motors Ltd - to exclusively look after the interests of car production.

*Top left: The HA Viva, the first Vauxhall to be built on Merseyside. **Above:** Just seven months after its introduction Ellesmere port sees the 100,000th HC Viva roll off the production line, the shortest time for any new car in the plants history prior to 1971. **Right:** The Chevette launched in 1975.*

One of Vauxhall's most famous pre-first world war cars, the immortal C-type Prince Henry, was first seen at the October 1911 Motor Show. War, however, soon intervened to interrupt the company's civilian car production. Vauxhall's 25hp D-type design of 1912 virtually became the British Army's standard staff car: almost 2,000 were built under Government contract. When King George V inspected the troops at Vimy Ridge it was a Vauxhall 25hp that took him as far across the Flanders mud as any wheeled vehicle could go.

After the war another 2,000 of Vauxhall's 25hp vehicles were sold for civilian use.

A new chapter began in December 1925 when the British company became a wholly-owned subsidiary of the giant General Motors Corporation. The deal, masterminded by GM's then president Alfred P Sloan Jr, gave the US company the entire ordinary share capital of Vauxhall Motors Ltd for a price of $2.5 million. As a result the Luton plant became GM's first manufacturing base outside North America - the first of many.

At the outset Vauxhall had competed in the top end of the car market, against such names as Rolls Royce and Bentley, but now the emphasis shifted to the mass market. In 1930 the company was producing only one model - the £750 23hp T-type Silent 80. By the end of the year the company was firmly in the under £300 market. By 1933 Vauxhall's Light Six was selling for only £215. The following year Vauxhall's annual production had risen to 20,000 cars, despite the terrible economic recession which gripped the world's, and the British, economy.

The second world war saw the Luton production lines given over to Bedford trucks, Churchill tanks and other military work. It was not until well into 1946 that civilian production could begin again. Even then the government decreed that export markets should take precedence over the home market.

Not until 1948 did any new models appear - the L-type Wyvern and Velox were the first of the firm's models to feature steering column-mounted gear sticks.

Increased demand for cars in the post-war years led to a major expansion programme at Luton. By 1950 a new 19.5 acre production building, erected at a cost of £14 million, was in use, although even this would soon prove to be insufficient to meet demand.

A real milestone in Vauxhall's history came in 1953 - the firm's Golden Jubilee - when not only did the company's output top 100,000 vehicles built in a single year, but also the company's' millionth vehicle also came off the line.

By then the Luton plant covered 800 acres and employed more than 13,000 people. In 1957 the first Victor arrived, the F-type 1.5 litre saloon, it quickly became Britain's top export car. That same year the sleek PA Velox and Cresta Sixes also appeared.

Top left: The first Cavalier built at Vauxhall, Luton. **Top right:** *Prime Minister John Major presents silver salver to Mike Chapman, Works Manager, which he received on behalf of all the work-force. The presentation was to mark Ellesmere Port's record output in 1990.* **Below:** *The new press shop, this-state-of-the- art Large Transfer Press carries out the work of four conventional press lines producing up to sixteen body panels per minute. Just 33 hours after the first piece of steel is pressed the finished car leaves the line, fully inspected and tested.* **Right:** *The new paint shop in 1991.*

Despite the massive expansion at Luton during the 1950s, and the moving of Bedford truck production to nearby Dunstable in 1955, Vauxhall needed still greater capacity. Hence in 1961 work began at Ellesmere Port.

The boom years of the 1960s saw Vauxhall recording ever-higher output figures. Its record 1964 figure of 342,873 vehicles was due largely to the introduction the previous year of another all new model - the HA Viva - a car which marked Vauxhall's re-entry to the one-litre class.

The 1970 London Motor Show saw the debut of the HC Viva - by July the following year the millionth Viva was rolling off the production lines at Luton: Viva 1,000,001 however was built at Ellesmere Port.

Other landmark cars were the Chevette, Vauxhall's first proper hatchback car and the first Cavalier saloon, both of which were launched in 1975 and which quickly became top ten sellers in the UK.

Despite severe recession and falling car sales in the late 1970s in the UK GM kept faith with Vauxhall and invested heavily in the company. Tangible evidence of that confidence appeared in 1980 with the launch of Vauxhall's first front wheel-drive car, the hugely popular Astra.

The Lotus car company became part of the Vauxhall group in 1987 - a marriage which led to the fabulous Lotus Carlton. In 1988 Vauxhall launched an entirely new Cavalier in two body styles, and 22 model variants, after a £122 million investment. A new Astra followed the new Cavalier into the showrooms in 1992. The following year however would be the year of the Corsa.

In the 1990s Vauxhall continued to invest vast sums in improving its UK production facilities, not least that £190 million engine facility at Ellesmere Port where 135,000 power units for the V6 Cavalier would be produced.

Meanwhile, by 1992, Ellesmere Port alone was producing more than 130,000 Astras a year.

Early in 1981 the increasingly close association between Vauxhall and Adam Opel, its sister company in Germany, resulted in the Vauxhall and Opel marketing organisations in the UK being combined as one operation. As a result smaller cars in the firm's range continued under the Vauxhall name while the larger cars adopted the Opel insignia and were sold alongside their Vauxhall equivalents.

Today, after four decades of production at its Ellesmere Port plant, Vauxhall Motors remains at the forefront of technical expertise; it also remains one of the region's principal employers. Above all however the Vauxhall Griffin logo remains one of the most recognisable brand images in Britain and around the world - and that is thanks to cars which not only bring back happy memories for millions of motorists but which still inspire them to return to the marque time and time again.

That same year saw the introduction of the car that did more for Vauxhall's fortunes than almost any other. This was the first front wheel-drive Cavalier, the J-type, which continued in production until 1988.

It was in 1983 that many believe that the Vauxhall renaissance really got into full swing - extra labour was being taken on, the firm's market share was increasing, annual sales rose to more than 250,000 and the recently introduced Nova was making great strides in the small car market.

The following year an all-new Astra made its debut, followed by the acclaimed new Carlton in 1986.

Top left: Staff celebrate the production of the first T85 Astra at Ellesmere Port, the home of the Vauxhall Astra. Above left: Quality review meeting. Below left: Assembly of the V6 engine. Below: The body framing-line where robots and people work together to form the complete body, 2003.

Throughout this time Vauxhall was investing both at Luton and at Ellesmere Port - a £90 million new paint plant went up at Luton in 1985, a £20 million improved paint facility was built at Ellesmere Port, as well as a further £9 million allocated to increase capacity at the northern plant. In 1985 Vauxhall/Opel registrations topped 300,000 for the first time in the UK.

Maintaining a name

The many large industrial enterprises which can be found on the Wirral provide employment for many thousands of local folk. And the great buildings which house those industries are modern-day cathedrals to enterprise. Yet though they may bear little physical resemblance to Britain's gothic medieval masterpieces those newer buildings share at least one distinctive characteristic with them: they need constant maintenance if their fabric is not to deteriorate.

Weather and time batter the structure of all buildings, not least those exposed to the climate imposed by our northern latitude and proximity to the Irish Sea. Almost inevitably then a corps of dedicated professionals has arisen to service industry's maintenance needs - and on the Wirral the best known name amongst their ranks is that of 'Moorcroft's', a company which has been pre-eminent in the area since the early 1960s.

But though the local story may have begun only in the 1960s the Wirral's Moorcroft Construction Company was in fact founded as long ago as 1934 by two men who at that time already sat on the board of a company known as Concrete Structures Ltd. The new company 'Moorcroft's' specialised in reinforced concrete, and its principal client was the London Borough Council for whom it became involved in the construction of deep underground bomb shelters prior to the second world war; in addition the new company also became heavily involved in the construction of

winding houses at pit shaft heads, along with coking plants for the coal mining and gas industries.

Following the ending of hostilities in 1945 Moorcroft's moved its operation to Luton in Bedfordshire which was also the UK home of the General Motors Corporation and its Vauxhall car manufacturing plant. Moorcroft's became one of the contractors to service the car plant by providing its building and maintenance requirements: the work was undertaken on a 'schedule of rates' contract. The company also became the maintenance contractor for other manufacturing plants belonging to General Motors in the area: the Bedford plant at Dunstable, and what was then AC Delco. When GM moved to Ellesmere Port in 1962 to build the new plant which would produce the Vauxhall Viva the Moorcroft Construction Company was one of the Luton plant contractors selected to provide the maintenance at Ellesmere Port too -a service which it continues to carry out to this day.

In 1976 Moorcroft's was acquired by another company, JA Elliott Ltd of Bishops Stortford, which had bought

Above: Moorcroft Construction's Telford Quay office.
Below, both pictures: Liverpool's Multiplex Cinema. Designed, built and fitted out by Moorcroft.

JA Elliott's first exposure to the perils of recession came when it lost £2.8 million on a London Docklands contract after the collapse of the client, the Kentish Property Group. At the same time banks were becoming increasingly cautious whilst a reassessment of value of Elliott's land holdings showed them to have decreased in value to a mere £27 million - down from £65 million just a couple of years earlier. On paper JA Elliott's was in fact insolvent. JA Elliott finally went into receivership on St Valentine's day, the 14th February 1991.

What did the collapse of JA Elliott mean for the future of 'Moorcroft's' now operating as Elliott (Northern) Limited and all those who worked for the company in Ellesmere Port? The two resident directors of Elliott (Northern) Ltd, along with three of the Group directors who sat on 'Northern's' board, managed to buy out the Ellesmere Port operation. The receivers simply wanted to sell to the highest bidder and it took time to convince them that Northern was actually solvent.

Moorcroft's with the intention of broadening its own client base in the North West and enabling it to become involved in the factory maintenance sector. Elliott's soon closed down Moorcroft's Luton operation but allowed the Ellesmere Port division to expand. With the demand for new commercial buildings and extensions required by industry in the boom years of the 1980s and early 1990s Moorcroft's continued to grow and became a major contractor with many new clients in the North West whilst still maintaining its core business of factory maintenance.

Towards the end of the 1980s the main board of Elliott's decided to change Moorcroft's name to Elliott (Northern) Limited; the idea behind this was that it would help enable the company to compete for larger capital projects under the banner of its parent company whose turnover was now in the region of £100 million a year.

The change of name proved to be rather badly timed: the company re-flagged, changed its name, colours and got new logos only for the parent company, Elliott's, to collapse.

Top left and top right: *Van Leer, their long standing relationship with Moorcroft Construction's has involved the Company with maintenance and capital projects at all Van Leer's Ellesmere Port sites.*
Above left: *Vauxhall's Ellesmere Port plant maintained by Moorcroft Construction since 1962.* ***Below:*** *Plan for the new paint shop at Vauxhall Motors, circa 1990.*

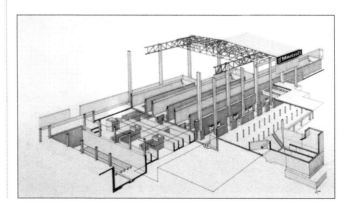

Happily the directors' bid was in any event the highest and was accepted.

Over the next two years Elliott (Northern) Ltd lifted its turnover to £17 million, expanding and even setting up a new division in the Midlands to cope with its increased client base. Unfortunately, although the aim had not been to go for quick turnover growth, it had been necessary to do so because of an agreement to service a monthly payment to the Receiver for the acquisition of the company. The cash flow position became intolerable however when payment on an substantial 'Interim Certificate' was delayed by the Home Office because of an internal reshuffle in its surveying department. This was ironic given that this was around the time that Prime Minister John Major was beating the drum on the subject of large firms jeopardising smaller ones by delaying payments due to them - a practice which the Prime Minister rightly said was prejudicial to the country's economic growth. John Major's exhortation's apparently went unheard at the Home Office. Northern's board of directors called in an insolvency expert for advice about how to deal with the situation and, acting on that that advice, called in the receivers on St Patrick's day 17th March 1993.

Throughout all the years, and quite apart from the ups and downs of take-overs, mergers, name changes and subsequent demises, the same workforce had been continuously carrying out the same maintenance work for the same companies. The clients' building supervisors still referred to the firm as 'Moorcroft's' and were very supportive of the Management Buy-Out by the two original resident directors Stuart Howard and Mike Lee

in 1993: they were also able to buy the shelved name of Moorcroft Construction Ltd from the receivers.

In April 1993 Stuart Howard and Mike Lee put 'Moorcroft's' back on the map along with 20 or so of the original Moorcroft men. The company now went back full circle to what its directors believed was its natural niche, providing building maintenance and cover to industry on a seven day twenty four hour basis. Today the now thriving company still directly employs all its own trades and labour as it always has done and by 2003 would consist of some 56 staff many of whom would have over 20 years service.

Top and above right: *Designed and built by Moorcroft, a swimming pool and sports facility for the Wirral Autistic Society who wanted a facility for their patients which would act as both a treatment area and leisure facility.* ***Left:*** *Drive pits and conveyer trenches for Vauxhall Motors.*

Although Mike Lee is a northern lad from Widnes, he began work as a joiner in Luton under his father Benny Lee who was a manager for Moorcroft's. When the Ellesmere Port car plant opened in 1962 Benny was the manager transferred by Moorcroft's to run the company's new Northern division and Mike tagged along to learn the business. Mike Lee had been joined by Stuart Howard in 1963; Mike already knew Stuart, both of them having served their time as joiners at ICI in Runcorn. Both Mike and Stuart were promoted through the ranks over the years and were elected to the board of directors by Elliott's after Benny Lee retired on his 70th birthday in 1980 - after having given some 46 years service to Moorcroft's.

In 2001 Stuart Howard decided to retire and sold his share of the company to Mike who over his 40 year career had now progressed from being a junior joiner just out of his time to becoming the owner of the whole company. Today Mike Lee remains the only original member of Moorcroft Construction Ltd, a company which he is passionately proud of - his only regret is that his father is not still alive to witness the unexpected course that events have taken.

Today, from prestigious offices at Maritime House, Telford Quay, Ellesmere Port, the directors and staff of Moorcroft Construction Ltd can look back over seventy years of corporate existence, and more than four decades on the Wirral. Those years have witnessed all the commercial vagaries which fate can throw at a business, yet, despite those many challenges, 'Moorcroft's' has survived to ultimately prosper.

Top and above left: Northern Scaffold Group Plc's factory, warehouse and offices all constructed by Moorcroft. *Below left:* Vauxhall's new paint shop during construction. *Below:* A 25 week contract completed by Moorcroft Construction in 1987, the listed four storey building built in 1890 by Thomas Telford at Tower Wharf, Chester, was converted into a Restaurant Bistro and Wine Bar .

Carbon is a girls best friend

Diamonds may be a girl's best friend, but as any schoolboy chemist will happily explain diamonds are just a form of carbon. And carbon is just a technical name for soot. Any Victorian entrepreneur who discovered a ready market for soot would have rubbed his hands with glee. In the 19th century one American businessman achieved exactly that; in the process he set in motion a chain of circumstances which would lead to the creation of an industrial facility on the Wirral which would produce many hundreds of thousands of tons of, albeit very special, carbon and surprisingly generate many millions of pounds in profits.

Cabot Carbon Ltd based at Stanlow, Ellesmere Port, came into corporate existence on 30th December 1948.

Made by the carefully controlled heating of 'residual oil' carbon black is a very fine, sub-micron particle with a complex shape. Today Cabot's central expertise rests on the efficient manufacture, conditioning and handling of those fine particles to meet a range of differing customer needs, such as the carbon black's reinforcement, conductivity and pigmentation properties. Cabot can produce carbon blacks with a combination of microscopic profiles and surface characteristics which its competitors struggle to replicate. Over the years the company has developed the technology to change both the 'morphology' and particle surfaces whilst at the same time increasing manufacturing efficiency.

The main application for carbon black is for reinforcement in rubber and for pigmentation in plastics, inks and coatings. Over 80 per cent of carbon black is consumed by the motor industry, mostly it is used in car tyres. A typical tyre will contain over one fifth of its weight of carbon black. Without that reinforcement a car tyre would wear out after just a few hundred miles.

Cabot Corporation is the world's leading carbon black manufacturer with significant market shares in each of the tyre, rubber, plastics, inks and coatings industries.

Top left: *Henry Siegbert, Deputy Chief of the American Economic Co-operation United Kingdom Mission breaks the sod at the site for the building of Cabot Carbon Ltd's new plant in Ellesmere Port.*
Below: *The official opening of the Plant on July 28th 1950 by President of the Board of Trade, the Right Honourable Harold Wilson, O.B.E., MP.* **Above right:** *A souvenir from the opening ceremony of the plant which was attended by 173 people.* **Right:** *Harold Wilson is given a tour of the plant.*

Stanlow or 'Stanlaws' history goes back to the Domesday Book when the land was owned by Earl Hugh Lupus a follower of William the Conqueror. In 1178 John, Baron of Halton and Constable of Chester, founded the Cistercian Abbey of Stanlaw but in 1279 the monks abandoned the area following fire and flood. The land was bought by the Manchester Ship Canal Company from the Marquis of Westminster in the 19th century.

The Shell Refinery at Stanlow opened in 1922 as a small tankage installation on the side of the ship canal at what was then simply known as Stanlow Point. The canal offered excellent water communications with the outside world and there were also outstanding road and rail communications links. Cabot Carbon Ltd would become just one amongst many world renowned names which today have an installation on this historical site.

It was back in 1882 that Godfrey Lowell Cabot and his brother Samuel built a carbon black plant at Buffalo Mills in Pennsylvania. Four years later Godfrey bought out his brother Samuel's interest in the company, a business which in the following years would move into both oil and gas development in addition to carbon black production. By 1897 Godfrey Cabot was able to claim to be the largest carbon black manufacturer in the USA — and in the world.

To build its new plant in the post-war Wirral the company was granted financial aid under the Marshall Plan.

The end of second world war had left much destruction all over Europe, not least in the United Kingdom. General George C Marshall the Chief of Staff of the US Army and later US

In the late 1940s Thomas Dudley Cabot (the son of Godfrey L Cabot co-founder of the parent company) had the foresight to investigate the possibility of building a carbon black plant in the United Kingdom, thus saving the UK government a great many dollars in foreign exchange: at that time this was the currency which had to be used to pay for carbon black. After much deliberation, and having looked at other sites such as Grangemouth, Milford Haven and Humberside, Thomas Cabot chose Stanlow because of its proximity to the Mersey and the Manchester Ship Canal where the heavy residual oil which is required to produce carbon black could easily be shipped. Until then all carbon black shipments came into the port of Liverpool from oil-fields abroad.

This page: Views of the plant circa 1950.

attended the opening ceremony which was held in the warehouse building where carbon black was to be stored

By 1950 there were some 70 employees who by Christmas of that year were producing carbon black at a rate of some 8,00 tons annually - the first high-abrasion furnace black ever to be made in the United Kingdom.

High Abrasion Furnace black or VULCAN 3 is used in compounds where abrasion resistance is required such as in car tyres. It was the most highly reinforcing form of black known at the time.

With slight operational changes the plant could also produce STERLING SO or Fast Extrusion Furnace black, a carbon with low heat generation properties used in inner tubes, cable sheathing and many other products such as boots and shoes.

Secretary of State proposed and then initiated what naturally became known as the Marshall Plan. This plan was an 'aftercare' programme lasting from 1948 to 1952 which enabled many industries within the UK and Europe to be rebuilt under the auspices of aid from the USA. That economic aid helped the UK and other European countries to return to normal economic life more quickly and restore world trade. General Marshall received the Noble Prize in 1953.

Work on Stanlow site began on 8th June 1949. Mr Henry Siegbert the then Deputy Chief of the ECA (European Co-operation Administration - the 'Marshall Plan') Mission to the UK performed the ceremony of breaking the ground on the site of the new plant in the presence of representatives of the Board of Trade, the American Embassy, and Simon Carves Ltd, the main contractors for the new plant.

The Stanlow plant was officially opened by future Prime Minister Harold Wilson, then President of the Board of Trade, on 28th July 1950. Some 173 people

Less than six months after the original unit was completed it was decided to add a second unit; this unit was completed in May 1953. A third grade of product, VULCAN XXX, was introduced in 1954, a grade of black which possessed exceptional electrical conduc-

*Top left: The Analytical Laboratory where samples from each batch are quality tested. **Above right:** On becoming a Borough in 1955 Ellesmere Port was presented with the Borough Mace, made of hall-marked silver gilt the mace was donated by Godfrey L Cabot, Inc., and Cabot Carbon Limited.*
***Right:** A Dunlop truck sets out with its load of carbon.*

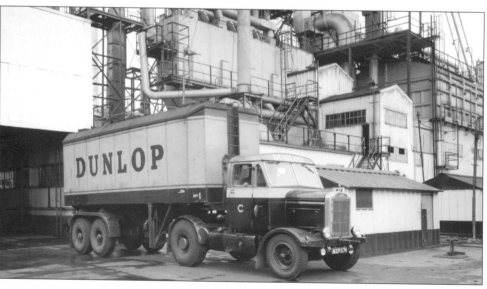

at Berre near Marseilles, Ravenna in Italy, Hanau in Germany, Botlek in Holland and Ciervana in Spain.

When the Stanlow plant celebrated its 50th anniversary on 28th July 1998 Thomas D Cabot's son Louis W Cabot, who was the first Managing Director of CCL in Britain, returned to join the Stanlow team and their families for this special occasion.

Historically the carbon black business has been very profitable. By the start of the 21st century that profitability was however eroding under the twin pressures of excess Western European carbon black capacity and low cost imports.

The carbon black market in the UK is declining as tyre manufacture migrates to central Europe. There are also large volumes of low-cost carbon black being imported into Europe from Russia and Egypt. For the company's 100 employees the firm's future challenge is to become significantly more cost competitive whilst also maintaining its technological leadership in its field.

Meanwhile, though some may still prefer diamonds, there's no doubt that carbon in other forms can be even more valuable - if only you know what to do with it.

tivity and which could be used in many anti-static products such as floor covering in operating theatres and for conveyor belts in hazardous atmospheres. VULCAN C and VULCAN 6 would follow. More units followed in quick succession: one in 1955, one in 1956 and one in 1957 in total raising the annual capacity to nearly seven times that of the original plant.

On 1st July 1959 the first British employee William M Fieldhouse, was employed as the company's Joint Secretary alongside his Boston counterpart FC Fernald, both looking after the affairs of Cabot Carbon Ltd. Bill Fieldhouse a former wartime army captain had joined the company as a chartered accountant on 1st July 1949. By 1979 by which time Bill Fieldhouse was Managing Director he had seen Cabot Carbon's original investment of $1,047,000 produce cumulative operating profits of $100 million!

Meanwhile, with the success of the Stanlow venture, the US parent company Godfrey L Cabot Inc went on to build further carbon black plants in Europe

*Top left, above and left: Manual packer and operators in the plant. **Below left:** The plant warehouse. **Below:** A birds eye view of the Stanlow plant.*

The first and the last

According to the old adage there are only two certainties in life - death and taxes. The very rich and the very poor may avoid taxes, but none of us avoid death. And if the manner of our passing may matter little to us once we are gone it is very important to those we leave behind.

Our loved ones want not only to see us end our days with dignity but also to see that their final farewells are made with fitting decorum. Until the 19th century however few funerals for ordinary folk left their mark. Our great churches and cathedrals were, and still are, filled with the effigies of, and memorials to, the great and the good, but most ordinary people had to be content with much less. For the average man or woman laying out would be conducted by a local woman, someone who was probably a neighbour who did this important job on a part time basis - and often doubled up as a midwife. The local carpenter would make a coffin and the burial in the local churchyard would, like as not, be marked with a simple wooden cross which would disappear in a few years' time.

The demand for elaborate funerals reached its height in the Victorian era, as witnessed by the many elaborate memorials in Britain's graveyards. And with that funerary elaboration rose the profession of the modern undertaker.

Few of today's firms of funeral directors were founded quite as long ago as the Victorian Age, but the family firm of Charles Stephens (Birkenhead) Ltd, with premises in Rock Ferry, Heswall, Neston and Bromborough, is a notable and honourable exception.

The firm was founded in 1896 by Charles George Rickard Stephens, helped by his wife Marie and just two employees. In 1993 the firm merged with another long-established firm of Wirral undertakers, that of Henry Norman.

*Above: Mr & Mrs L C R Stephens. Mr Stephens joined his fathers firm in 1928 at the age of seventeen. **Below:** A Victorian view of Conway Street around the time Charles Stephens established himself as a Funeral Director.*

Charles Stephens originally hailed from Plymouth where he had worked as a shipwright before moving to the Wirral in the 1880s to work for Cammel Laird. In 1896 Charles set himself up as a funeral director and carriage master at 44 Conway Street, Birkenhead, with additional stables in Raffles Road.

Four years later the sombre business of undertaking was shaken by an extraordinary event .

That Earth-shaking event happened across the Atlantic in the brash state of New York, that melting pot of fashions and cultures where very innovation was instantly celebrated with the lighting of fat cigars. In the city of Buffalo, New York a man had been carried to his grave in a motorised hearse!

Across the world funeral directors in their trademark top hats and black tailcoats noted this development with as much disdain as shock. That unseemly innovation attacked the very roots of a profession in which tradition was held to be almost sacred.

In Britain, as elsewhere, the profession's straight-backed, stiff upper-lipped decorum was symbolised by the slow and muffled trot of the Belgian Black ponies whose passage was always greeted by raised hats of respect as they high-stepped down the road to the graveyard.

When the news that a motorised hearse had been used in New York state it must surely have caused a shudder to pass through the dignified frame of Charles Stephens too at his funeral parlour in Conway Street.

Charles had only been in the profession half a dozen years. Should he now embrace this new method of carrying the dead? Would his potential clients want to make their final journey behind an internal combustion engine? The answer was simple - no. In the end Mr Stephens

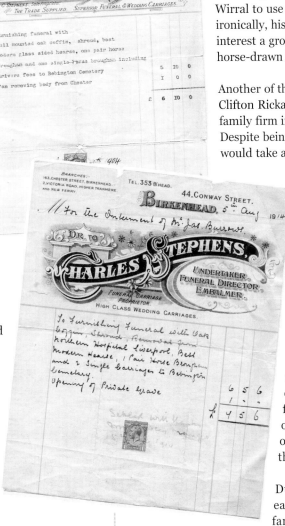

decided to keep faith with his horses. Other firms however soon came to believe that the future lay with motorised hearses. In 1909 the first motor hearse in Britain was constructed by Poppe and White for the firm of Pargetter's of Coventry.

Meanwhile, until his death in 1928, Charles Stephens continued to travel to the continent and buy horses there before bringing them back to the Wirral to be trained.

It was not until the 1930s that the founder's son, a second Charles Stephens, began phasing out the horses in favour of Minerva cars - and in the process becoming the first funeral director on the Wirral to use a motorised hearse. Today, ironically, his nephew is now noting with interest a growing trend for reverting to horse-drawn hearses.

Another of the founder's sons, Lewis Clifton Rickard Stephens, had joined the family firm in 1928 at the age of 17. Despite being in a reserved occupation he would take a commission in the Royal Navy when war broke out in 1939. Charles Stephens, joined the marines after the second world war.

Lewis' mother would keep the business running during the war when understandably the firm was very busy. It was however difficult to survive because money was not readily available, as a consequence much of the firm's business was carried out on trust, with relatives only settling their bills after the war had ended.

During the 1930s, 1940s, and early 1950s two other families, the Highfields and the Matthews, would work as chauffeurs and assistants helping ensure that the

This page: *Receipts from 1904 (top) and 1914.*

Stephens family business would prosper after the austerity of the immediate post-war years.

Lewis Stephens, who returned to the business after his service during the war, died aged 89 in 2000. He had conducted his final funeral just a few months before his own death.

Lewis' son, Jeremy, would become the third generation of the Stephens family to head the business.

The continuing family line is assured by Jeremy's daughter Gemma Henderson-Stephens who already works in the business. And she has young twins Patrick and Thomas to continue in her footsteps should they choose to do so - though whether they will ever see black ostrich-plumed horses drawing a hearse still remains to be seen.

Parked on the forecourt of the company's headquarters at Clifton House, Bebington Road, Rock Ferry where the firm moved in 1965, is a sleek new hearse. The building is named after the ward of the old Birkenhead Council which the elder Charles Stephens, the former shipwright at the Cammel Laird shipyard and later prominent freemason, once represented as a Tory councillor and alderman.
The vehicle is an extended Daimler with

a V8 engine. It cost about £77,000. In the back it has a deck in walnut veneer for carrying the coffin, and it has an underdeck for flowers. There is also a wreath rail on the top. All the glass is toughened for safety reasons.

The casket is pulled from the back along rubber rollers. Inside there is also a wheeled bier for use in those churches or other premises not equipped with their own trestles on which to rest the coffin.

Work to stretch and modify cars for use in funerals is carried out by a number of coach-building firms in the North of England, including Eagle Specialists of Bolton who

Top: An ancestor of the Stephens family with a horse drawn hearse. ***Above right and right***: A funeral directed by the firm in 1922.

polished coffin with heavy mouldings, an engraved inscription plate and a silk faced dressing gown robe with silk frilling and interior to accord'. For obvious reasons the dressing gown robe has always been important to loved ones of the deceased, and swansdown was favoured by many.

And in addition there would be a motor hearse and staff in attendance at the house or hospital for removal to the chapel of repose. In 1971 the new grave accounted for just £15.20 of the cost.

are owned and operated by the Wilcox family of Chalfont St Peter, Buckinghamshire.

Charles Stephens uses a modern hearse for just three or four years and then changes it for a new vehicle. By that time it will have travelled around 35,000 miles.

An idea of the increases faced by funeral directors is given by the £8,889 bill for a 1975 Daimler hearse finished in Carlton grey with black Ambla upholstery.

The cost of cemetery plots, at around £600 to date, have also been increased greatly and are now the most expensive part of a funeral.

By contrast back in 1899 Robert Gallienne, also of Conway Street, whose firm was to later to merge with Charles Stephens, was charging nine pounds, eight shillings and sixpence (£9.42) for a service which included a zinc plate-lined oak coffin, a Washington hearse, two broughams, three cabs and the cemetery fee.

Even in 1971 the cost of a funeral was a mere £87.55. For that you would get a 'best-

Top left and right: Charles Stephens' impressive fleet in the 1970s.

Jeremy Stephens, whose company now employs 37 people, pays silent testimony to a youth during which he was expected to learn the skills of his profession the hard way.

In the philosophy of the Stephens family there was no question of a son moving from the school desk to the leather swivel chair of the boss without an intervening period of real work.

You have to be physically fit to be an undertaker according to Jeremy. 'My father wouldn't think of me doing any office administration work until I was

competent in all other aspects of the business which would include valeting and washing the vehicles and transferring loved ones from hospitals and nursing homes. Jeremy studied to become a qualified embalmer with the British Institute as well as being a member of the Royal Society of Hygiene.

sial introduction of motor hearses. 'Funerals were stately sedately, nobody rushed' says Jeremy. 'A horse and carriage was dignified. At first motorised hearses were thought by many to be an abomination. There was a slow transition around the late 1920s and early 1930s, but once motorised transport generally became more familiar they too were accepted'.

Again according to Jeremy the work was distressing to begin with... 'but when you are brought up in the business you tend to be drawn into it. You are aware of what goes on. You hear your father going out very early in the morning. You are conditioned. You know what is expected of you'.

Today funerals are very different from those arranged by Jeremy Stephens' grandfather before the controver-

Above: The funeral of Harriet Hough affectionately known by the people of Neston as 'Mrs Neston', directed by Henry Norman and Charles Stephens in 1997.
Below and right: The firms premises in the 1960s.

As many readers will recall, for a long time after their introduction the motor hearses would travel at a respectful 10 mph, though never as slowly as the horses who were specially trained to lift their forelegs slowly. But of course today's hearse drivers have to deal with very different traffic conditions.

Do people still lift their hats when the cortege passes? There is less respect than there was Jeremy Stephens believes. 'Life is 100 miles an hour now, but you still get the older generation standing and raising their hats. We may be in the jet age, the space age, but we still retain the dignity and respect for death'.

Today the staff of Charles Stephens includes six fully qualified funeral directors, all members of the British Institute of Funeral Directors; in addition four members of the British Institute of Embalmers are also employed. Though not a formally designated training centre the staff willingly share their techniques with funeral directors from overseas, taking students not only from the continent but even from as far away as Africa.

The firm's centenary in 1996 was celebrated by the sponsoring of certain roundabouts in the Wirral area with flowers. In addition the firm also sponsors the Lyceum brass band in Port Sunlight

Today this family business remains committed to the vision of its founder, the first Charles Stephens, of providing the very best of funeral services. Every member of the Charles

Stephens team is dedicated to offering the best possible service, help and support to the firm's clients.

During the course of more than a century the firm of Charles Stephens Funeral Directors has been providing the people of the Wirral with the kind of funeral they would wish for themselves and for their loved ones. Wirral folk are not mawkish or over sentimental, but they do have a long tradition of giving death the quiet respect it deserves and of marking that final transition with due dignity. Generations have trusted Charles Stephens and his family with making those arrangements - and none have been disappointed with the professional and understanding manner with which the firm has provided this, the last service of all.

Top left: New premises at Neston.
Left: Directors of the firm, back row left to right, Steven Belmar, Ralph Peters and Andrew Deighton and front row left to right, Jeremy Stephens, Richard McDowell and Gemma Stephens.
Below left: One of Charles Stephens Daimler limousines.
Below: Charles Stephens' Clifton House, Rock Ferry premises.

Roll out the barrels

Today New Chester Road, Rockferry is home to one of the Wirral's most enterprising businesses: Staniford (Rockferry) Ltd. The name gives strangers no clue to what the business does: it, and its associated company Air Sea Containers Ltd, are however one of the United Kingdoms best known suppliers of steel drums and other specialist packaging.

Herbert Staniford (1906-1998) and William Gaskell (1896-1967) were both born into coopering families.

Richard Staniford, Herbert's father was a first generation cooper and became foreman at the cooperage of John Bibby & Sons Seedcrushers in Liverpool.

The Gaskells were also a coopering family. William's father had left Liverpool to work in Northwich and William was born near there.

In 1900 William Gaskell senior brought his family back to Liverpool where he worked as a 'wet' cooper.

William junior served his apprenticeship at Mannings Cooperage in Liverpool; he worked at the Mersey Cooperage in the years between the wars before moving to Hartley's where he met his future business partner Herbert Staniford.

In the 1930s Herbert Staniford was foreman cooper at Hartley's Birkenhead depot in Beaufort Road.

One of the main jobs at the cooperage was to repair and clean 90 gallon Australian tallow casks. The full casks arrived at Birkenhead docks and were then delivered by steam powered lorries to Lever Brothers in Port Sunlight. There the casks were emptied and returned to Hartley's for repair and cleaning before being sold to the Irlam Soap Works near Manchester.

Hartley's moved to Liverpool around 1937, leading to Herbert and William meeting for the first time.

Top left: Co-founder Herbert Staniford. Above right: Founders Herbert Staniford and William Gaskell with their first company vehicle. Right: Loading barrels.

Needing extra money to support their young families the pair moved to Liverpool's Stanley Warehouse in 1944. The Essential Work Order in place during the war however meant that Herbert had to first attend a tribunal when Hartley's objected to him leaving.

The pair went to work for the American Army which was shipping large amounts of goods and equipment through Liverpool from the USA as part of the build up for the Allied offensive in Europe. Most of the goods arrived in wooden crates which the Americans insisted only coopers be allowed to open.

In October 1945 Herbert and William started work at Shell's detergent plant at the Stanlow refinery mending barrels used to carry a detergent paste. Shell was experiencing serious problems attracting good coopers from Liverpool because of the travelling time.

Taking a chance Herbert and William pointed out to the Shell management that in their opinion Shell would never get enough good men to travel to Stanlow and that the solution was to move the barrels to the coopers. They explained that they were both well known in coopering circles and had the experience to start a business on Merseyside. To the pair's surprise and delight Shell backed their idea and in January 1945 gave them a contract to repair a large number of barrels, even thought they had no premises nor employees.

Top left: Staniford & Gaskell's coopers talk shop.
Centre: A Staniford & Gaskell letterhead.
Right: Don Staniford, followed his father as Managing Director of Staniford (Rock Ferry) Ltd.

Fortunately it became possible to sub-let part of the derelict old Mersey Cooperage on New Chester Road, Rock Ferry. At first there was no electricity or water but the two partners set to work.

With the help of Tom Boggie, the manager of the Midland Bank, they opened an account and visited a solicitor to establish a formal partnership agreement.

Shell arranged all the delivery and collection of the barrels, and even hand delivered payment cheques once a month. The cheque for the first month's work was for £100 and one shilling: not bad when a average journeyman cooper's wage at the time was just £19 per month.

The firm's first coopers were soon employed: Patrick Sarsfield, George Woods, Ivor Jennings, Don Mackie, Phil Taylor, Henry Boniface and Jimmy McHale. The firm's output increased threefold in the second month of operations.

The business grew quickly and after several years the firm also began to clean and repaint 45 gallon steel drums. Labourers were needed for this task and the workforce grew to twelve coopers and eight unskilled men. In 1949 the partnership bought its first lorry, a Fordson Thames for £622. Its driver would be Ronnie Mulvihill who had once worked for Herbert Staniford at Hartley's. Eventually becoming the works maintenance fitter Ronnie would not retire until 1986 after a 51 year long association with Herbert Staniford.

Staniford & Gaskell Ltd
COOPERS & DRUM RECONDITIONERS
VATS, CASKS, BARRELS ETC. MADE & REPAIRED FOR BREWERS, DISTILLERS, SHIPPING, OIL & CHEMICALS
24" New Chester Road
ROCK FERRY
BIRKENHEAD

Herbert's son, Don Staniford who would one day be Managing Director of Staniford (Rockferry) Ltd, had good cause to remember Ronnie Mulvihill and that Fordson lorry. As an 11 year old schoolboy he would sometimes go with the lorry to collect barrels. One collection was from the Cadbury factory in Bournville. Ronnie reversed the truck up to a stack of barrels awaiting collection and went off to find some help. The barrels all contained powdered milk and when the driver returned he found a terrified schoolboy trapped in the cab with the windows totally blacked out by swarms of wasps attracted by the milk: Don was rescued by Cadbury's workers who hosed the wasps away.

During its first six years of trading the partnership had show a three-fold increase in business on its first year, with Shell accounting for 90 per cent of turnover. However in 1952 there was a sharp decline in the use of barrels although it would not be until 1961 that the last consignment of wooden barrels would be delivered to the Teepol plant at Stanlow.

Alloy drums replaced barrels for detergents after 1952; although expensive they could be reused many times: the metal drums were constructed with protective steel rolling hoops and their bodies did

Above: Once known as Manor Farm, the old District Bank in Greasby was acquired by the company and opened as Manor Farm Restaurant in 1972.
Right: Greave Dunning.

not often suffer badly from denting or distortion. Initially expensive machinery was not needed to process the drums for reuse and Staniford and Gaskell were able to recondition them to the required standard.

However there was trouble ahead: the partners had not invested in up to date steel drum reconditioning machinery and the steel drums the partnership was able to produce were only suitable for filling with low grade products.

In December 1958 the firm, recently having wisely become Staniford & Gaskell Ltd to offer limited liability to its partners, was given the bad news that Shell was to phase out the use of alloy drums and replace them all with steel. Lacking the equipment to meet the required standard the new company lost the Shell contract. In eight of the eleven years between 1952 and 1963 the business lost money.

In 1964 William Gaskell was almost 68, ten years older than his partner, and wanted to retire. Herbert's Staniford's 25 year old son Donald, an industrial chemist who worked for Shell at its Stanlow laboratories, persuaded the Midland Bank, with some difficulty, to lend him and his father the £1,600 needed to buy out William Gaskell's share of the business.

Starting work in April 1964 Donald injected a new air of enthusiasm into the business, quickly seeing that more than £4,000 was invested in a new office building and an automatic drum scrubbing machine.

Midland Bank and, taking a deep breath, asked for an unsecured loan of £100,000 - more than a million pounds at 21st century values. Astonishingly the bank agreed.

The next ten years were ones of hard work and continuous improvements. A new automated plant was able to produce high quality reconditioned drums at a rate of one every 25 seconds - 1,000 a day - ten times the output in 1963, yet manned by only eight operatives.

In 1969 the company took on a new name Staniford (Rock Ferry) Ltd, following which Don bought 50 per cent of the business.

As result of that relatively modest investment income tripled over the next four years. Work was taken on from George Prendergast Ltd when that company ceased trading in 1967; its manager William Stunzi came to work for Staniford & Gaskell. Burmah Oil became a new customer, accounting for 40 per cent of production.

By 1968 the firm was confident enough to negotiate the purchase of its premises for £14,000 which until now had been leased.

Much more investment was needed however to buy equipment. Don Staniford went to see the manager of the

The company's second big break came in 1970 when Shell-Mex and BP awarded it 'Open Order' contracts for as many 'grade one' drums as it could produce.

Top: Part of the Staniford fleet outside the company premises in the 1970s. ***Above:*** *Opening day of Greave Dunning December 1981, pictured (from left to right) are Boddington Director and Head Brewer, Ralph Warwick, Nell Staniford, Herbert Staniford, Anne Staniford and Don Staniford.*

Herbert Staniford retired in 1971 leaving his shares to his five children - which gave Donald a controlling interest of 60 per cent. Don's brother Douglas Staniford joined the company in 1973, he had previously worked in the then new field of computers at the Royal Insurance in Liverpool; he soon took charge of the increasingly complex administration systems. Brother-in-law Tadeus Stawiarz joined in 1974: both would become directors in the 1970s.

The period 1964 to 1980 saw the income of the company increase 60-fold. This enabled diversification into other business ventures which included boat building and property restoration to develop both a restaurant and a public house.

Diversification into the restaurant business had begun in 1971 when the rundown District Bank building in Greasby village had been acquired on leasehold. Once known as Manor Farm the house had been built in 1680. Manor Farm Restaurant opened for business in October 1972.

The Manor Farm Restaurant would continue in business until 1983 before being leased out to other operators as the Barngrove restau-

Top left: Presentation of the 'Cheshire Life' Restaurant of the Year award in 1982. Above right: Douglas Staniford, brother of Don Staniford, who joined the company in 1973. Right: Don Staniford at The Launching of 'Katharos', August 1986. 'Katharos' is being lowered onto the deck of the floating crane 'Samson'.

rant. In the mid 1990s it was leased to Peter Horsley the Barngrove's former manager who would subsequently run this business as 'The Manor'.

In 1977 Staniford's also acquired Ashmount Farm, adjacent to Manor Farm, paying £25,000 at auction. It was decided to convert the farm into a public house - if a liquor licence could be obtained. Getting a licence was far from easy: objectors included some local residents, the Temperance Society, the nearby Catholic church, the Licensed Victuallers Association and Whitbread's Brewery.

The application looked doomed, but Staniford's were not about to go down without a fight. A petition signed by hundreds of local people in favour of the application was produced, whilst magistrates were shown the plans of the area which revealed that 334 new homes had

been built in the area in recent years and that another 900 were due to appear. The clincher however came from local character Stan 'Taffy' Higgs who was being examined by the barrister for Whitbread's brewery which then had a monopoly in the area. Sensing some antipathy to Whitbread's the barrister asked Taffy if

accommodate Air Sea's expanding operation. Staniford (Rock Ferry) Ltd's principal activity, drum reconditioning, entered a difficult period in the 1990s with the introduction of cheap, non-returnable drums. By the end of the decade, the industry had contracted sharply and out of 15 Merseyside reconditioners in operation at the start of the 1980s, 14 had closed down. Staniford's was able to survive the downturn because of financial security provided by it's other interests and the support of Air Sea Containers which had seen tremendous growth through out the 1990s.

In October 2003, the future of the drum reconditioning industry on Merseyside was assured when Stanifords completed a joint venture agreement with the largest operator in Europe, Blagden Packaging N.V. The new company, Blagden Staniford Packaging Ltd, is to invest £1,000,000 in the Birkenhead operation to increase capacity of the existing plant. When completed in early 2004, the factory will produce 10,000 drums per week and will be, by far, the largest reconditioner in the UK.

he didn't like the taste of Whitbread's bitter. In his best country yokel manner Taffy raised a howl of laughter in the court by replying 'I wouldn't say that your 'honour' - it hasn't got a taste!' No doubt others would disagree with Taffy's opinion, but his wry comment was enough to ensure that Staniford's got the licence they sought for what would become their Greave Dunning public house.

All that was needed now was to build the new pub. An opportunity to obtain the necessary authentic materials presented itself when Saint Barnabas' Church in Rock Ferry was made redundant by the Church of England. Staniford's obtained the contract for its demolition and transported sandstone blocks, hand-made bricks, wooden pews, stone flags, oak doors and roof trusses to Ashmount Farm for use in the construction of the 'new pub'. The Greave Dunning opened in the midst of a blizzard on 14th December 1981. The pub would become one of the most popular on the Wirral. The Greave Dunning would be operated by its builders until 1988 when it was eventually sold to Bass Brewery, who had made an offer that could not be refused.

Nine years earlier, a separate company, Air Sea Containers Ltd, had been formed by Don Staniford in response to new legislation governing the transport of dangerous goods. This company grew rapidly and in 1997 Staniford's, once again, turned property developer building a new 25,000 sq ft warehouse on its 2 acre site in Price Street to

Above: Staniford's, 1978.
Below: Air Sea, 1999.

Bath time

How old do you have to be to recall having a bath in a tin tub in front of a coal fire? Perhaps not as old as many might think. Even as late as the 1970s many British houses still lacked a bathroom and folk were still faced with the choice of going along to the municipal baths or heating up water on the stove.

For youngsters it was always an opportunity for fun, even if soap invariably ended up in your eyes. Perhaps soap was stronger then - it certainly ought to have been since we all got a lot dirtier then in the days before smokeless fuels.

And how many times did mother fill the bath? Just the once of course, with children lined up in ascending order to get their weekly dip.

As for those more intimate memories. How many readers recall the having their backs scrubbed by a loving spouse?

But that's nostalgia for you. We remember the good bits and forget the bad. How many mothers got sick to death of heating up endless buckets of water and carrying them to the bath? How many of us complained about the entire house getting damp from the steam? And, if you were hot on one side from the fire, what about the other side which always seemed to be freezing?

The truth is that all those who had no bathroom gave a great cheer on the day they finally had one installed. But who to get in to do the job? There have always been large national firms ready to take on such work by the thousand, but such firm's are unlikely to offer customers much in the way of a personal service.

Happily there is somewhere in the Wirral where customers can find the kind of service and care seldom encountered elsewhere: Roberts & Co. based in Argyle Street Birkenhead.

Way back in the days when Queen Victoria was still on the throne the Kennedy family founded the business, then trading as the Birkenhead Metal Warehouse, at

107 Argyle Street. Originally the firm traded as a metal merchants and brass founders; it was subsequently bought by the Walsh family and would branch out as a plumbers merchants as well as into selling fireplaces to discerning customers.

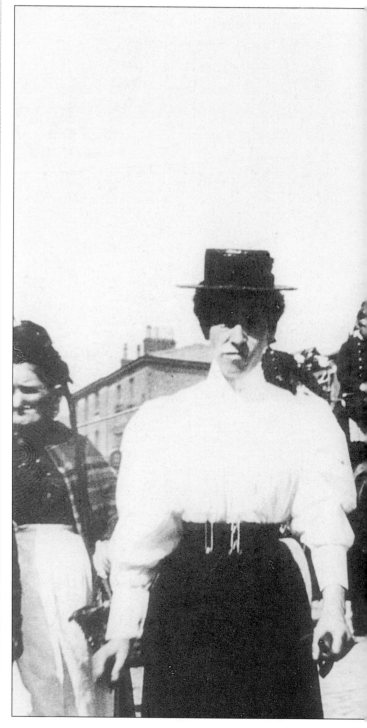

Right: Roberts & Co. (trading as the Birkenhead Metal Warehouse) around the turn of the twentieth century.

With its seven staff, and a handcart for making deliveries, the firm would be a major success with Birkenhead residents, a success based on a reputation for a personal service and experienced staff which would only be enhanced over the following decades.

The years since the shop first opened have seen many changes, not least ever increasing plumbing standards and water regulations emanating from Europe; meanwhile staff have endeavoured to be ever more helpful to clients, not least in offering a first rate design and installation service.

In 1984 Roberts went through a major upheaval to make life easier for customers by demolishing a shop on Grange Road East to form a car park and collection point for clients. Previously customers had to attempt to load up by negotiating the terrors of Argyle Street with its double yellow lines, nearby bus queues and, more often than not, heavy traffic too.

By the 1990s expansion was underway with a project to join together premises at 107, 109 and the recently acquired 111 Argyle Street - the latter an impressive structure of red brick overlooking the town centre.

The facade of the original premises would be demolished and rebuilt in keeping with the elegant frontage of 111 to help create a single store designed in the architectural style of the early 20th century.

The expansion and refurbishment would be made possible thanks to the co-operation and financial support of the Wirral's Department of Planning and Economic Development which provided a grant to help increase business, more job opportunities and in general to stimulate regeneration amongst local businesses.

Sales and storage areas almost doubled as a result of the new development, allowing the plumbing and central heating departments, together with builders and hardware and tools departments, to be extended.

The whole of the first floor covering some 2,500 sq ft would now be devoted to display of bathroom suites, showers, ceramic tiles and accessories.

Some of the suites on show would for the first time demonstrate working jacuzzis (which incidentally have absolutely nothing whatsoever to do with French writer Emile Zola's famous headline 'J'Accuse' in the notorious Dreyfus case but are named after the Italian-American inventor Candido Jacuzzi) whirlpools and spa baths with power showers and body jets demonstrating the features of a relaxing hydro massage

Expansion over the years has enabled the company to offer a large range of products more competitively. Today's owners of the firm's long history and their ten staff aim to continue to provide customers with unrivalled choice and advice, and to extend Roberts' acclaimed installation service.

A regular visitor to Roberts is the 'professional DIY-er', someone who is prepared to tackle quite large and complicated jobs, something which modern products make practical when helped by the advice and genuine expertise from on-hand Roberts & Co.'s highly trained staff who include amongst their numbers, time-served plumbers and central heating engineers.

Fabulous products and competitive prices have given Roberts an edge over its competitors, particularly over the 'sheds' - the DIY superstores which are perceived as cheap but, which when looked at more closely, seldom live up to the promises promoted in their national adverts.

Above: The company's first motorised vehicle.

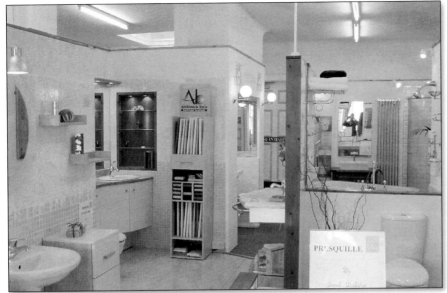

quality products and supported by some of the industry's major manufacturers. The six year warranty on workmanship is even transferable when customers sell their homes so creating a valuable asset.

The most exciting and impressive feature of all however remains the Roberts bathroom showroom with its outstanding display of bathroom suites - it's all a far cry from those long gone if happy day when a tin tub in front of the fire was the order of the day. No doubt many visitors to Roberts showrooms will remember with more than a twinge of nostalgia those now far off days when they once bathed in front of a roaring coal fire; but though many will recall those long gone happy days few will in truth regret their passing as they admire the most modern and impressive bathroom fittings available today.

Meanwhile, although traditional time honoured personal service is still a prominent feature at Roberts, modernity has its place too: a computerised point of sale for the showroom is only one aspect of a sophisticated computer system which contributes to a finely tuned smooth running business by controlling their stock and providing fast and vital information for their accounts department and management.

Staff loyalty has been something of tradition at Roberts. The former Managing Director Harry Walsh retired in 1973 at the age of 75 after having serviced an incredible 60 years with the company - not only that, it wasn't his first job!

Meanwhile at the start of the new millennium, in order to offer customers even more peace of mind, Roberts would launch its own ABTA-style guarantee in conjunction with IBSA the Independent Bathroom Specialist Association - the additional comfort of knowing that their deposit and installation is in safe hands and will be carried out by IBSA approved fitters. For total confidence when paying a deposit on new bathroom equipment the deposit is now covered by an independent insurance backed guarantee -just like your holiday is guaranteed by ABTA. If IBSA approved fitters are used then their workmanship is also covered free of charge. On completion customers will be given a no cost six year warranty from IBSA. IBSA is a group of independent retailers in the premier division of the UK's bathrooms industry selling only top

Leading brands from Europe and the UK provide today's consumers with the very latest in technology and design. Bathrooms these days are no longer just functional they have become leisure rooms with the very latest state-of-the-art gadgets imaginable. Roberts and Co. have two floors of showrooms with over 80 displays to choose from and a wealth of experience to satisfy the most demanding fashion conscious and discerning bather.

This page: *Roberts & Co.'s showrooms in Argyle Street, 2003.*

Tools of the trade

Looking for ironmongery, hardware, handtools, power drills, engineering tools, or even janitorial supplies? Wirral residents needing such things naturally make a beeline for Old Chester Road in Great Sutton to the premises of TE Hughes Ltd.

The business was founded in 1961 by Tecwyn Hughes and Peter Robbins. The firm initially traded under the name RH Trading, though shortly afterwards the founders renamed it Robbins & Hughes Ltd.

Tecwyn and Peter had met whilst working at Henry Wright Ltd of Ellesmere Port where Tecwyn was the General Manager and Peter the Sales Manager.

Tecwyn 'Tec' Hughes had left school at the age of 14 and went to work for HS Tiltson Ltd, an ironmongers in Dock Street, Ellesmere Port. Tec worked there for seven years before leaving to do his National service in the RAF at the age of 21. Two years later Tec returned to Tilston's: just twelve months after his return the proprietor died. The business was bought by Henry Wright Ltd and Tecwyn was made manager. For the next five years Tec worked for Henry Wright Ltd alongside Peter Robbins before the intrepid pair decided to set up a business for themselves.

Naturally Tec and Peter's new business was as ironmongers and engineers' merchants. To begin with there was just Tecwyn and Peter together with an assistant running the office. At its height however the company would grow to employ 40 people.

Top left: *Founder, Tecwyn Hughes.*
Below: *Robins & Hughes Ltd in the 1960s.*
Left: *Priory Cottage, the company premises in the early 1970s.*

The first premises were in Ellesmere Port's Queens Street where Tec and Peter paid a rent of £1 a week. A year later they were advised that the M53 motorway was scheduled to run through their premises and they moved to the former Bradley's outfitters in Station Road. The building was far larger and accommodated 10 staff.

The company had been promised 30 years on the new site, but once again new roads made a move necessary. In 1972 the Old Farm, Priory Cottage in Great Sutton village was purchased; at the same time a small shop, previously James & Co, in Warrington was acquired. A smaller shop in Whitby Road near the train station in Ellesmere Port was also bought in order to maintain a presence in the town centre.

During the 1970s and 80s the company became a major supplier to all types of industry in the North West region.

A purpose-built warehouse was erected for the needs of the ever expanding business on the Rossmore Industrial Estate in 1978, which became the head office.

By this time however, due to illness, Peter Robbins no longer had any involvement in the business. Tec's son-in-law Stuart Charnley joined the company in June 1986 and son David Hughes in November 1988.

In 1988 Tec retired, selling the core business at Rossmore to competitors Buck & Hickman, though passing on the original business at Great Sutton and Warrington to his son David and to son-in-law Stuart. The company name was changed at this time to TE Hughes & Son Ltd.

In 1993 TE Hughes & Son Ltd acquired a power tool sales and repair centre in Manchester.

When Tec Hughes sold the Rossmore business, however, competitive retraints were imposed which made trading difficult for some time. Increasing competition from national chains, superstores and Internet trading during the 1990s from both home and abroad in a decreasing market also caused difficulties.

Happily however, turnover has been maintained in recent years, despite prices to the customer, especially of power tools, having fallen by up to 25 per cent. Though prices may be lower the company has been selling more goods and maintaining its position in the market place.

Keeping its position has in part been due to the company's willingness and ability to supply any quantity, small or large. Staff are always willing to attempt to meet any special requirements and to offer advice and help at any level. The company also takes pride in holding an excellent range of items in stock.

The customer is the firm's first priority; its staff aim to provide a unique service that is accessible, speedy, efficient and friendly to all.

Today TE Hughes Ltd deals with anyone from the man in the street to multinational corporations and is now even enjoying some limited trade with Europe.

Top left: Robbins & Hughes Ltd, Rossmore Industrial Estate, 1980. ***Above left:*** *A view inside Robbins & Hughes Ltd in the 1980s.* ***Below:*** *T E Hughes & Son Ltd, 2003.*

Acknowledgments

The publishers would like to thank

Birkenhead Central Library

Liverpool Central Library

Andrew Mitchell

Steve Ainsworth

True North Books Ltd - Book List

Memories of Accrington - 1 903204 05 4

Memories of Barnet - 1 903204 16 X

Memories of Barnsley - 1 900463 11 3

Golden Years of Barnsley -1 900463 87 3

Memories of Basingstoke - 1 903204 26 7

Memories of Bedford - 1 900463 83 0

More Memories of Bedford - 1 903204 33 X

Golden Years of Birmingham - 1 900463 04 0

Birmingham Memories - 1 903204 45 3

Memories of Blackburn - 1 900463 40 7

More Memories of Blackburn - 1 900463 96 2

Memories of Blackpool - 1 900463 21 0

Memories of Bolton - 1 900463 45 8

More Memories of Bolton - 1 900463 13 X

Bolton Memories - 1 903204 37 2

Memories of Bournemouth -1 900463 44 X

Memories of Bradford - 1 900463 00 8

More Memories of Bradford - 1 900463 16 4

More Memories of Bradford II - 1 900463 63 6

Bradford Memories - 1 903204 47 X

Bradford City Memories - 1 900463 57 1

Memories of Bristol - 1 900463 78 4

More Memories of Bristol - 1 903204 43 7

Memories of Bromley - 1 903204 21 6

Memories of Burnley - 1 900463 95 4

Golden Years of Burnley - 1 900463 67 9

Memories of Bury - 1 900463 90 3

Memories of Cambridge - 1 900463 88 1

Memories of Cardiff - 1 900463 14 8

Memories of Carlisle - 1 900463 38 5

Memories of Chelmsford - 1 903204 29 1

Memories of Cheltenham - 1 903204 17 8

Memories of Chester - 1 900463 46 6

More Memories of Chester -1 903204 02 X

Memories of Chesterfield -1 900463 61 X

More Memories of Chesterfield - 1 903204 28 3

Memories of Colchester - 1 900463 74 1

Nostalgic Coventry - 1 900463 58 X

Coventry Memories - 1 903204 38 0

Memories of Croydon - 1 900463 19 9

More Memories of Croydon - 1 903204 35 6

Golden Years of Darlington - 1 900463 72 5

Nostalgic Darlington - 1 900463 31 8

Darlington Memories - 1 903204 46 1

Memories of Derby - 1 900463 37 7

More Memories of Derby - 1 903204 20 8

Memories of Dewsbury & Batley - 1 900463 80 6

Memories of Doncaster - 1 900463 36 9

Nostalgic Dudley - 1 900463 03 2

Golden Years of Dudley - 1 903204 60 7

Memories of Edinburgh - 1 900463 33 4

Memories of Enfield - 1 903204 14 3

Memories of Exeter - 1 900463 94 6

Memories of Glasgow - 1 900463 68 7

More Memories of Glasgow - 1 903204 44 5

Memories of Gloucester - 1 903204 04 6

Memories of Grimsby - 1 900463 97 0

More Memories of Grimsby - 1 903204 36 4

Memories of Guildford - 1 903204 22 4

Memories of Halifax - 1 900463 05 9

More Memories of Halifax - 1 900463 06 7

Golden Years of Halifax - 1 900463 62 8

Nostalgic Halifax - 1 903204 30 5

Memories of Harrogate - 1 903204 01 1

Memories of Hartlepool - 1 900463 42 3

Memories of High Wycombe - 1 900463 84 9

Memories of Huddersfield - 1 900463 15 6

More Memories of Huddersfield - 1 900463 26 1

Golden Years of Huddersfield - 1 900463 77 6

Nostalgic Huddersfield - 1 903204 19 4

Huddersfield Town FC - 1 900463 51 2

Memories of Hull - 1 900463 86 5

More Memories of Hull - 1 903204 06 2

Hull Memories - 1 903204 70 4

Memories of Ipswich - 1 900463 09 1

More Memories of Ipswich - 1 903204 52 6

Memories of Keighley - 1 900463 01 6

Golden Years of Keighley - 1 900463 92 X

True North Books Ltd - Book List

Memories of Kingston - 1 903204 24 0

Memories of Leeds - 1 900463 75 X

More Memories of Leeds - 1 900463 12 1

Golden Years of Leeds - 1 903204 07 0

Memories of Leicester - 1 900463 08 3

More Memories of Leicester - 1 903204 08 9

Memories of Leigh - 1 903204 27 5

Memories of Lincoln - 1 900463 43 1

Memories of Liverpool - 1 900463 07 5

More Memories of Liverpool - 1 903204 09 7

Liverpool Memories - 1 903204 53 4

Memories of Luton - 1 900463 93 8

Memories of Macclesfield - 1 900463 28 8

Memories of Manchester - 1 900463 27 X

More Memories of Manchester - 1 903204 03 8

Manchester Memories - 1 903204 54 2

Memories of Middlesbrough - 1 900463 56 3

More Memories of Middlesbrough - 1 903204 42 9

Memories of Newbury - 1 900463 79 2

Memories of Newcastle - 1 900463 81 4

More Memories of Newcastle - 1 903204 10 0

Newcastle Memories - 1.903204 71 2

Memories of Newport - 1 900463 59 8

Memories of Northampton - 1 900463 48 2

More Memories of Northampton - 1 903204 34 8

Memories of Norwich - 1 900463 73 3

Memories of Nottingham - 1 900463 91 1

More Memories of Nottingham - 1 903204 11 9

Bygone Oldham - 1 900463 25 3

Memories of Oldham - 1 900463 76 8

Memories of Oxford - 1 900463 54 7

Memories of Peterborough - 1 900463 98 9

Golden Years of Poole - 1 900463 69 5

Memories of Portsmouth - 1 900463 39 3

More Memories of Portsmouth - 1 903204 51 8

Nostalgic Preston - 1 900463 50 4

More Memories of Preston - 1 900463 17 2

Preston Memories - 1 903204 41 0

Memories of Reading - 1 900463 49 0

Memories of Rochdale - 1 900463 60 1

More Memories of Reading - 1 903204 39 9

More Memories of Rochdale - 1 900463 22 9

Memories of Romford - 1 903204 40 2

Memories of St Albans - 1 903204 23 2

Memories of St Helens - 1 900463 52 0

Memories of Sheffield - 1 900463 20 2

More Memories of Sheffield - 1 900463 32 6

Golden Years of Sheffield - 1 903204 13 5

Memories of Slough - 1 900 463 29 6

Golden Years of Solihull - 1 903204 55 0

Memories of Southampton - 1 900463 34 2

More Memories of Southampton - 1 903204 49 6

Memories of Stockport - 1 900463 55 5

More Memories of Stockport - 1 903204 18 6

Memories of Stockton - 1 900463 41 5

Memories of Stoke-on-Trent - 1 900463 47 4

More Memories of Stoke-on-Trent - 1 903204 12 7

Memories of Stourbridge - 1903204 31 3

Memories of Sunderland - 1 900463 71 7

More Memories of Sunderland - 1 903204 48 8

Memories of Swindon - 1 903204 00 3

Memories of Uxbridge - 1 900463 64 4

Memories of Wakefield - 1 900463 65 2

More Memories of Wakefield - 1 900463 89 X

Nostalgic Walsall - 1 900463 18 0

Golden Years of Walsall - 1 903204 56 9

More Memories of Warrington - 1 900463 02 4

Memories of Watford - 1 900463 24 5

Golden Years of West Bromwich - 1 900463 99 7

Memories of Wigan - 1 900463 85 7

Golden Years of Wigan - 1 900463 82 2

Nostalgic Wirral - 1 903204 15 1

Wirral Memories - 1 903204 747

Memories of Woking - 1 903204 32 1

Nostalgic Wolverhampton - 1 900463 53 9

Wolverhampton Memories - 1 903204 50 X

Memories of Worcester - 1 903204 25 9

Memories of Wrexham - 1 900463 23 7

Memories of York - 1 900463 66 0